From Ops Center to Industry: Lessons from the Arena of Leadership

Three-hundred Years of Cumulative Military & Industry Experience

Kevin Lewis

www.lmkpartners.com

Vision Spots Publishing
A Service Unit of LMK Partners LLC

Copyright Information Page

Kevin M. Lewis
CEO/Managing Partner
LMK Partners LLC
8647 Richmond Highway, # 636, Alexandria, VA 22309
www.LMKPartners.com
Info@LMKPartners.com

First Printing, 2013

ISBN-13: 978-1484148143
ISBN-10: 1484148142

Printed in the United States of America

Contents

Preface

*A*rena: a sphere of interest, activity, or competition; a place or situation for controversy

If ever there was a domain characterized by competition and controversy, it is the domain of leadership. Leaders, whether they lead large or small organizations, regularly face these challenges. They live in a glass house. They are always in the arena.

This book extracts lessons from those who have faced challenges within the leadership arena. They will impart to you not only what they have learned but also how to effectively raise up the next generation of leaders.

Many books exist on the varied aspects of leadership and leader development. However, in my opinion, nothing takes the place of sitting down and talking with someone who has lived it, who is not afraid to speak of failures, and who will speak candidly on what emerging leaders today must be prepared to face.

Thank you for parting with your financial resources in the purchase of this work. I trust that by the time you are at the other end of this book, you will have gained new and valuable insights from the lessons within.

Kevin. Lewis
Christian, Husband, Father, and Author

Foreword

We have all been inspired by outstanding leaders – parents, teachers, coaches, team captains, commanders, politicians. They have motivated us to reach beyond our expectations and achieve results we never thought we could attain. We have also been disappointed by leaders who failed to inspire us or take risks which allowed us to exceed our competition.

Leadership is about communicating goals to others through verbal, written, and physical means and motivating them to achieve results which meet or exceed those goals. The 21st Century has given us numerous means to communicate beyond the written and verbal methods of the past – the internet, mobile phones, streaming video, to name a few. The physical environment extends from harsh deserts, to deep undersea waters, and to space. Kevin Lewis, through conversational interviews with military leaders who have retired and moved on to careers in the commercial world, provides us insights into overcoming the challenges presented to 21st Century leaders.

LTG (Ret) Bill Campbell recounts entering a locker room as an undersized football player and reading the plaque on the wall from a retired coach, "He took them all, big and small, and molded men." Bill led the Army in fielding the tactical internet and went on to become a leader in international business.

MG (Ret) Dorian Anderson reminds us to"Operate outside your comfort zone". Dorian, a retired Infantry officer now runs his own consulting firm, providing counsel in areas well outside the realm of an Infantry Soldier.

LTG (Ret) Glenn Webster tells us that "Leadership is about trust…It goes both ways". Glenn ("Fuzzy" to his friends) led the 3d Infantry Division in Iraq and the 3d US Army in Iraq and Afghanistan and now teaches leadership to senior executives in the Department of Defense, earning their trust while learning from them.

Kevin Lewis has given us a book which demonstrates different perspectives on leadership and thoughtful ideas on how to deal with 21st Century opportunities. He informs us through these interviews that our Nation continues to develop superb leaders to deal with the pace and challenges of the world we live in. We can be thankful for these leaders and Kevin's engaging conversations with them to illuminate our thinking.

Paul J. Kern
GEN, US Army (Retired)

Paul J. Kern, GEN, US Army (Ret) is a Senior Counselor with The Cohen Group. He served as President and Chief Operating Officer of AM General from August 2008 through January 2010 and is currently a Director with ITT, ITT-Exelis and iRobot Corporation, and a member of the CoVant Board of Managers. Since retiring from the Army in 2005, he has held the Class of 1950 Chair for Advanced Technology at West Point, was a Vice President for Battelle, and a Director on the Anteon and EDO boards.

GEN Kern retired after almost 38 years with the US Army as the Commanding General of the Army Materiel Command. In June 2004, the Secretary of Defense tapped GEN Kern to lead the military's internal investigation into the abuses at the Abu Ghraib prison in Iraq, a compelling assignment that he handled with integrity and resolve. In 1996-97 he was the Commanding General of the 4th Infantry Division, Mechanized, where they developed the organization, tactics, techniques, and equipment implemented in today's networked force. In 1991 he led the 2d Brigade of the 24th Infantry Division in the attack into Iraq. He began his career commanding operational units as a platoon leader and troop commander in the Blackhorse Regiment in Vietnam.

GEN Kern graduated from West Point in 1967 with a Bachelor of Science degree. He holds Master Degrees in Civil and Mechanical Engineering from the University of Michigan and was elected to the National Academy of Engineering in 2006. He was a National Security Fellow at the J.F. Kennedy School, Harvard

University and is currently a member of the Defense Science Board. He has a unique career which blends technical expertise, combat operations, program management, policy development, and advisor to senior political leaders.

Introduction

Leading people...that is one of the greatest challenges any individual will undertake...and will likely be one of life's most gratifying experiences when one succeeds. But what does it mean to be a successful leader? To quote a prominent leadership coach, "What does successful leadership look like?" In the following pages we hope to bring you an answer...a set of views that make up the leadership collage begged by this question.

In building this collage, we determined that we needed to first identify an organization or institution wherein high risk and high reward play significant roles and reach out to those willing to go on the record and discuss their views on effective leadership. This would require us to reach out to a group of leaders who have been tested in multiple settings addressing a broad spectrum of challenges. The institution determined to reflect such a level of risk and reward is the U.S. military...and the leaders to whom we reached out is a group of retired military flag officers now serving in industry. We conducted interviews with each of eleven men who rose to the rank of general or admiral and later transitioned into a new season of civilian leadership.

Capturing their experiences as military and civilian leaders brings a rich and in-depth view of the challenges and issues that leaders face. This combined with their own philosophies and approaches help to paint that successful leadership collage.

The backgrounds of these men include combat arms, logistics, engineer, information technology, cyber-security, and intelligence. They have been stationed around the globe, spanning the spectrum of experience from military command to policy and doctrine formation. They include a former Chief Information Officer for the Army, a former commander of "Patton's 3rd Army", an inductee into the West Point Army Sports Hall of Fame, and a naval officer called back to active duty directly by the President to oversee infrastructure construction projects in Iraq. Currently they all serve in industry either as business owners or corporate executives.

The core interview template was the same for each. We dedicate a chapter to each interview with the objective of keeping the content conversational and personal. The topics include approaches to raising up leaders, an effective leadership culture and how to impact it, organizational impediments to leader development, communications in the current viral age of social media, and reflections on lessons learned. Although the core questions are essentially the same, each interview brings its own unique and personal viewpoint. Where appropriate, the author inserts a note where his personal experience with the interviewee adds helpful background. Our overall goal is to provide you with a real life view of leadership perspectives from people who have been faced with difficult, sometimes high risk, decisions. Our hope is that these perspectives, which span views from a military operations center to the open business marketplace, will enhance and complement you professionally, personally and serve as a means by which your organization, no matter how large or small, can benefit.

Acknowledgements

This effort would not have been possible without the contributions of these 11 men. They were enthusiastic about making themselves available and to go on the record to give their personal thoughts and insights. We are extremely grateful to each one of them.

Maj. Gen. (ret) Dorian Anderson
Maj. Gen. (ret) Guy Bourn
Brig. Gen. (ret) Albert Bryant
Lieut. Gen. (ret) William Campbell
Maj. Gen. (ret) James Coggin
Maj. Gen. (ret) David Fastabend
Maj. Gen. (ret) Steven Hashem
Rear Adm. (ret) Peter Marshall
Rear Adm. (ret) David Nash
Maj. Gen. (ret) Gregory Schumacher
Lieut. Gen. (ret) Glenn Webster

Each interview is a standalone chapter, at the beginning of which is a summary of each contributor's background.

Chapter 1:
Celebrate...Outside of Your Comfort Zone

Dorian Anderson
Former Commanding General
Human Resources Command, U.S. Army

Meet Dorian Anderson, Major General (ret) now operating his own management consulting business serving the Federal/Defense market. Dorian has studied, lived, taught, and discussed leadership for over four decades. A graduate of the United States Military Academy at West Point New York, he served 30 years in the US Army holding leadership and command positions at all levels as an Infantry Officer, culminating as Commanding General, US Army Human Resources Command located, at the time of his retirement, in Alexandria, VA. Following his retirement from the US Army, he served as a Business Unit Vice President for a major defense firm and founded his consulting business.

He earned a Bachelor of Science degree from the United States Military Academy at West Point, NY, and a Master of Arts in Management from Webster University. He is a 1995 graduate of the US Army War College at Carlisle Barracks, PA and a graduate of The Executive Program at University of Virginia's Darden Business School. He recently became a 2012 inductee into the West Point Army Sports Hall of Fame.

AUTHOR NOTE: I have had the privilege of recently working with Dorian on a series of business development efforts. His calm, steady-handed approach through stressful and uncertain situations has been a hallmark of his leadership style.

Dorian, thanks again for being available for this effort. As organizations strive to meet their mission and to continue to grow, it is critical that senior leaders raise up new leaders. What do you see as the core responsibilities for senior leaders in raising up that next generation of leaders?

Well, the core responsibility is foundational and it goes all the way back to what leaders do. To summarize it in one word, "influence". Leaders influence by showing the way, by providing the resources that allow for realization of the organizational vision, goals, and objectives, and then encouraging those accountable to perform and improve themselves. Leaders really have to establish an environment, a culture that is constantly improving and building on success. The senior leader provides a way; a senior leader provides or makes available the necessary resources; and a senior leader is personally involved. In addition, if you do those three things, I think that you will find that the organization will run better. You will have a crosscutting view on what is going on inside the organization, and then you will see an amazing thing happen. You will see natural leaders emerge. Now there are some not suited for leading in that environment, but may be suited to leading in another environment. As such, you will create a generation that will carry on your legacy by immolating and building on the senior leader's leadership example.

You just touched on something that pertains to identifying people or looking at people as potential leaders. There are some people who are just either not suited or just do not want to be in leadership positions. They just want to be individual contributors. There are others of course who are most suited for the role of leader. What do you look for in an individual that would bring you to believe that he or she is someone that you can grow as a leader?

Growing leaders requires a deliberate plan and daily activity that include establishing conditions for growth and a set of standards. I recommend a reference that summarizes the criteria. The first reference is the Maxwell Leadership Bible New King James Version, Copyright 2002, and the second is a book entitled "Business by the Book" by Larry Burkett, Copyright 1998. These references point to the basic characteristics that I am looking for in leaders – whether they are emerging or experienced. You are really looking at the potential of this person at a foundational and enduring perspective. Do they have the character for being a leader? Are they committed? Can they communicate? Are they competent at what they are doing and do they have courage? We are not talking about a 'yes' person and not necessarily a rebel either, but a person who is not afraid to speak what they know and believe in a supportive tone and not rebellious in nature. Are they just starting? Do they focus? Are they generous? Do they take the initiative? Do they listen? Do they have a passion for what they are doing? Are they positive? Moreover, have they demonstrated the ability to solve the problems?

Are they responsible? Do they know themselves? Do they demonstrate self-discipline? Do they have a servant's heart? Are they teachable? Do they have a vision? How do they get along with their peers? If they have people working for them, how do they handle the people that are working for them? Do they have a charisma that draws not only people to themselves, but also draws the best out of everyone who surrounds them? Now, that is what I look for when I am looking at someone who is going to be a potential leader.

Allow me to inject a thought here. I recall when we spoke previously that your office played a vital role during the Pentagon 9/11 crisis. A crisis brings out many things in people and organizations. As you look back at that experience, what did you learn about people responding in a crisis and the leadership skills that you felt were truly needed to be sure the mission was accomplished?

I lost my Senior Rater (my boss's boss) during that time and three great Americans from our Command. We had to quickly and deliberately focus the command on the most important task at that point in time. The most important thing at that time was security, security of the people physically, mentally and spiritually. For example, we had quite a few people with children in daycare. We let them go to take care of their families. We said, "Go and take care of your family. Go home - we will call you."

After establishing security – of the building, of the families, and of the data we focused on gaining accountability. We had plenty of volunteers, we had a rehearsed COOP plan, and we had both formal and informal leaders emerging and providing guidance, and ideas, appropriately, deliberately, and calmly. We were able to account for everyone in the Army assigned to and visiting the Pentagon. That was about a three-day venture, 24 hours a day. Simultaneously, our Casualty and Mortuary Affairs Branch went into full gear and executed their very difficult and sensitive mission professionally and with an amazing calm and professional demeanor. I could go on and on. Our organization came together, adjusted work schedules and priorities, and executed portions of our continuity of operations plan. We had to take action. We did not have time to sit around and worry or be afraid. Then we had to open up a space to accommodate the Army's G1 staff to enable them to work in an alternative location.

We pushed to get everyone synchronized on what we were doing. It was not just to do the work – Army business did not stop. I watched healing happen while we were responding to the emergency. There actually was therapy in getting people to focus on the task at hand. This prevented mental deterioration. As they were performing their duties, they were taking care of one another.

5

Communication was paramount. It was very difficult. Early on, the phones did not work. Therefore, we determined a way to establish how to communicate. We had a contingency plan and we actually pulled the plan out and executed it. What I saw were people that I could depend upon. I was convinced that our internal assessments of who we brought into the command and our training programs were validated as a result of the emergency of 9/11. I saw some heroes emerge; the people you would not think would take that extra step – stepped up. Yes, these types of situations do tend to bring out the best in people <u>who were well led in healthy environment.</u>

Those are very insightful observations. Thank you for allowing me to throw that curve ball to you. Real leadership shows up in that people rise to the occasion when such critical events occur. On a day-to-day basis, we realize that our lives do not exist in a critical event world. For most of us, we are pushing through what we might call a normal set of events as we strive to accomplish our mission. As organizations move through these events, they can miss the mark in raising up leaders. For some organizations, blindspots exist. As you look out at organizations today, where are organizations missing the mark when it comes to raising up leaders? What are they not doing that they should be doing or what are they doing that they should not be doing?

As we compare military leadership with business leadership there are differences, but the principles are the same. The demand on leaders and the needs of the led are the same. Organizations in both the military and in business are made up of people, and people need to be led. One of the things that you find in under-performing organizations in both the military and in businesses is that they fail to invest in their people. Let me define "invest", because investment is not always just money. Investing requires a plan. Investing is spending time with, providing benefits for, making learning opportunities available, and expecting a return on the investment by holding them responsible for the improvements expected because of the investment. They fail to invest because they do not have a plan. If they do have a plan, it may not be articulated; and if it is articulated, it may not be reinforced as a part of the day-to-day operations.

Every day leadership is more than managing data, more than managing the profit and losses, more than managing business development, and more than managing training schedules and service delivery. It is managing the people by paying attention to their needs. Leadership includes recognizing strengths and how to best use their strengths in regards to the organizational needs. As the senior leader, you must make sure you are closely in tune with all aspects of the organization.

In the Army we are taught the importance of having 360% awareness and security. Everyone on the team has a 'sector' to watch. However, often, you will find there are organizations lacking in this area. Their people may all be looking in the same direction or in no direction at all. The senior leader really has to create that environment that establishes that 360° sensibility. When you have an organization that routinely pays attention to all aspects of the organizational performance then raising up leaders becomes a habit.

Let me share a thought here and get your response. I remember reading a study about the new soldier coming into the Army. The business world is experiencing the same thing. It is this new generation of young people coming in, digital natives, young people who are growing up in a world far different in terms of technology, in how they collaborate, and in how they communicate than you and I did. As such, the culture and environment of an organization can contribute to or hinder leadership development depending on how it relates to this new generation. How can senior leaders adjust to be sure they are tuned in to the culture and be more effective in drawing upon new leaders that are coming out of this new culture?

First impressions are lasting. How you bring people into the organization sets the tone for an organizational culture. It is critical to convey to each person joining the team how their position is in relationship to the rest of the team, the performance expectations, and importance of teamwork. You must make sure that they have every opportunity to succeed and that the necessary tools for success are available to them. You set the tone by how you act every day, how you react as a senior leader to various situations, and how you treat your people. In all organizations, the truth in the culture is found in the rating and evaluation system. The performance evaluation will drive your conduct and your culture. How you 'on board' and how you evaluate reflects what is important in the organization.

Institutional knowledge in any organization is important. Some people keep their knowledge close to the vest. What are your thoughts on how that institutional knowledge can be better shared, better utilized?

That is a hard one. You have heard the cliché "power is knowledge" or "knowledge is power". Leaders ought to ask themselves "Can my team perform when I am not there?" or, "Do I have a piece of knowledge that is critical to the operation that I have not shared with anyone?" If the answer is yes, then the leader has potentially become an impediment to organizational success. Our next breath is not promised. If critical knowledge or information is unavailable or being withheld it is difficult for any organization to operate effectively.

If, on the other hand, you are disseminating information, you need to ensure both dissemination and <u>compliance</u>.

Institutional knowledge written into standing operating procedures (this is the way we do things around here) that are current and understood by all the people in the organization contributes to high performance and efficient use of time.

Communications today is rapid. It is real time. It is dynamic. It is again a different world for younger people today. Some of the senior people are having difficulty dealing with this new environment. How can we get senior leaders today that are raising up leaders in that next level down to prepare

themselves better in how they communicate? What would you say to a room full of young aspiring leaders as to how they should be communicating and how should they be conducting themselves in that environment?

I would say the first thing you must do is to go and check your own heart. The 21st century is really exciting. A transparency has emerged in this 'information age' and this transparency is long overdue. People who have not adjusted to the transparency of this age are the ones who get in trouble when they think they are not on 'the microphone.' Today, you are always on the microphone. Also, things that are in your heart will come out of your mouth. We have a multitude of technical tools available to help us better communicate. What we choose as a primary communication device or method is a personal matter. Senior leaders must become aware and learn to function in a transparent environment.

However, with all of the technical advances, on principle has not changed - treating people with dignity and respect. It is a biblical principle found in Matthew 7:12, New International Version (NIV), "so in everything, do to others what you would have them do to you, for this sums up the Law and the Prophets." Further in Luke 6:38 "Give and it shall be given unto you" or in other words, what goes around comes around.

Communications and personal conduct are on display unlike any other period in history. Successful communications and personal conduct are about treating people right. For senior leaders and emerging leaders, if you practice treating people right, even when you have to exact discipline, the result will be that you will impact them not out of meanness or as a personal attack, but out of correctness – correcting actions. Then you will find that people will give you back exactly the same attitude you give them. This applies to written communications as well. In today's world, whatever you write now can go global in moments. Whatever you say can be recorded and it can go global in a moment. Therefore, it is critical to have a heart towards being authentic, respecting people, and treating all with dignity and respect. Why? Because what is in the heart will come out of the mouth, show up in actions and attitudes.

Let me pose a personal question. We are all our own worst critics. We go through life and we can look back and Monday morning quarterback all our decisions and everything we have ever done. If you could take a step back, look at your past, and possibly change anything, what changes might you have made or what types of things might you have done differently or different approaches might you have taken?

The major thing I would change would be my attitude. In order to change that attitude, the first thing I would do is focus and commit spiritually (accepting Jesus Christ as my personal savior) early on, and stay the course. I look back and recall that there were too many distractions where I wasted my energy. The second thing would be to change my attitude towards authority. The leadership that we came under as junior officers was often harsh, often negative. It really did breed contempt. I realize now that I did not have to do it that way. Authority is the divine principle and how I

11

reacted to authority resulted in how authority reacted to me.

What advice would you give to a room full of leaders who have the mission of raising up the next generation leaders? What would you charge them to do?

The first thing I would say is, "Hey, celebrate the opportunity in raising up others. That is a good thing and you can have an impact on others' lives." Secondly, be diverse. Go outside of your comfort zone. Do not just raise up people that look like you or with whom you are comfortable.

I believe God put each person here for a purpose and gave each person skills for that purpose. Pay attention to the current set of people on your team and invest in them. Then finally, for the senior leader, assess your program. What you personally check becomes important to your team. Is it doing what you expected it to do? Are you seeing any outcome and impact or are you just seeing data?

Data versus outcome. That is an excellent point. One other question: what is in the future for Dorian Anderson? What are you looking to do now? What are some things that you are pursuing?

The current environment is very interesting and challenging. There are opportunities out there and I want to be sensitive to those and make sure I am positioned right for those for the right reason. I am at the will of the Lord God and I believe He is sending me back into the business world. Therefore, there are interviews, there are people to continue to talk to, and there is life to enjoy every day. You know there is a verse that says, "This is the day that the Lord has made, now we will rejoice and be glad in it." So what is in my future? I will continue to do what I do - encouraging all those around me, staying engaged in business activities, and enjoying all the 21st century has to offer.

Dorian, I want to thank you for your service to our country and to this effort. New leaders are going to benefit greatly from your candid insights.

Thank you, Kevin, I am honored for this opportunity to share my experiences.

Chapter 2: They Will Remember...and the Memory Will Not Be Neutral

Guy Bourn
Former Commanding General
III Corps Artillery, U.S. Army

Meet Guy Bourn, Major General (ret), now serving as an executive in the defense aerospace industry. Guy is Vice President, Defense Systems, Washington Operations for Alliant Techsystems (ATK), a premier aerospace and defense company with more than 17,000 employees and revenue in excess of $4.3 billion. Guy and his business development team are responsible for coordinating and supporting all business development activities in the Washington, DC area for ATK defense-related products.

Guy was commissioned a second lieutenant in the field artillery after graduating from West Point in 1974. During his 30-year career in the Army, he commanded at every level from Lieutenant to Brigadier General. His last command position was as the

Commanding General of the III Corps Artillery at Fort Sill, Oklahoma. He also served as the Special Assistant to the Assistant Chairman of the Joint Chiefs of Staff. In that capacity, he traveled with the Secretary of State for two years. His last duty assignment was Chief, Office of Military Cooperation in Cairo, Egypt. Guy retired from the U.S. Army in 2004 as a Major General to accept a position as Vice President of the Sokhna Port Development Company, the first private company to manage a seaport in Egypt. After three years in that position, he returned to the United States to join the ATK team. Guy holds an undergraduate degree in General Engineering from West Point. His Master's degree in Systems Technology is from the Naval Postgraduate School at Monterey, California.

Guy, let me thank you again for participating in this project. Let's move right into this. It is vital for organizations to grow and meet their missions, meet their objectives, and to raise up new leaders. What do you see as the core responsibilities for senior leaders to make that happen?

My experience is that the corporate world doesn't do a very good job of that as a corporation. It seems to me that an awful lot of upward mobility and leadership training is actually done by the individual. We used to say, when we were in the Army, that you are your own best personnel manager and your own best career manager. What I see in the corporate world is that an executive is his own best career manager and his own best leadership manager. He builds his own leadership resume by moving from job to job and developing leadership and management brands.

Having said that, I think the responsibility of any leader, though, is first to set the example and then communicate a value set within that organization. The leader is responsible for articulating what the values of that company or that organization are and then living them himself or herself, setting clear goals for that company and for the personnel within. Even if subordinates are not being groomed for higher positions, they should still have goals that they've set and are expected to meet. There is also a responsibility for all leaders to ensure that their company or organization advocates good citizenship whether it would be supporting community groups or participating in local politics or non-profit organizations that help with the community in some way.

There are some people who are satisfied being technical contributors all their careers and then there are those who want to move up, who want to take up that mantle of leadership. What do you look for in an individual who is the latter? What would you want to see in them in order for them to succeed as a leader?

They have to be confident in their abilities. People are reluctant to follow someone who doesn't have any confidence in themselves. I think a leader needs to be compassionate. They need to understand that people have needs and desires; that they have problems that need to be resolved. You've got to show some compassion. It doesn't mean that you have to coddle them but I think you do have to demonstrate a certain sense of compassion. Everybody has a cross to bear of some kind. If a leader doesn't understand this, then they are pretty naive. Everybody has problems of some kind and some are worse than others. Some handle their problems differently.

Nonetheless, you as a leader need to have some sense of how to connect with people. You also want leaders to have common sense which is not very common. They've got to have a sense of what's right and wrong. There are many people that just simply do not have that. Not to be discouraging but at times those who are focused solely on the technical aspects of their work have blindspots in this area of applying common sense. They've got great talents in technical areas. But they don't seem to have the common sense to apply to different situations which, I believe, is the primary reason they don't want to serve in a leadership capacity. They are very comfortable in a technical area and that's fine. They just don't seem to be able to apply the common sense to areas outside their particular comfort zone of technical expertise. To be regarded as a rising leader, a person must be dedicated to whatever they are doing and it needs to show relatively early in their performance.

One other thing is appearance. And when you start talking about this, it can often seem superficial and not very important. But the fact of the matter is that your appearance can help, if not be a big part of, your effectiveness. As a leader in the military we look at how well they wear the uniform, how clean it is, how neat it is. In the civilian world, we note how someone dresses, can they dress appropriately for the particular occasion, do they come in with holes in their clothes, wearing dirty sandals; how well do they groom and take care of themselves. How is their posture, does it project confidence? If they don't take care of themselves, physically, mentally, spiritually, they are probably not going to take care of their subordinates very well. And, again, I realize that this may be dismissed as too superficial. But, I believe it's true. Small things like this matter. They serve as indicators.

Organizations believe that they need to be doing the right thing but often times they miss the mark when it comes to raising up leaders. They'll talk about it, there will be policies in place but sometimes they just miss it. How do you see organizations missing the mark? What are they not doing that they need to be doing when it comes to grooming that next set of leaders?

Mentorship is something that I don't think companies do very well. They don't realize that they can have a very positive impact on growing their leaders. But, to do so, they've got to mentor them. Senior people should share their experiences. And by senior, I don't mean older people necessarily. I'm talking about people with experiences that the subordinate doesn't have and the senior can share. Actually that goes both ways too. Often times a subordinate may have experiences that a senior doesn't. Mentorship should really go both ways. The military seems to be pretty much senior-driven down. But I've seen in the corporate world it can go both ways. You can actually mentor your boss. That, of course, can be a pretty delicate thing to do. But it can happen. It can be especially true of a boss who has come in from another company and tries to apply things in the new company that aren't very effective. One of his subordinates with a certain amount of aplomb may be able to mentor the senior and explain why that particular technique may not work for reasons that the new boss may be totally unaware. A senior should be open to that type of subordinate outreach. But again it's got to be handled delicately.

This issue feeds into and speaks to the culture of an organization. A report not long ago was published addressing how the Army is absorbing digital natives, that whole new generation of young soldiers coming in that grew up in a totally different world from today's senior leaders. Their life experiences, technology, how they communicate will impact how they relate to and connect with an organization. This speaks to how the culture of an organization has to adjust in order to begin to raise up those leaders. As you've transitioned from the military into the business world, you are dealing with many issues that touch on culture and how organizations work. What are you seeing as some of the cultural issues that organizations have to be thinking about when they are looking into raising up those younger leaders?

I've actually thought a fair amount about this and I'm not sure I have a very good answer. For example, there can be two companies whose missions are quite similar but their cultures are quite different. One might focus on nothing but the bottom line. Bottom lines are important. There is no getting away from it. But if the ethical standards are fairly weak, the bottom line may suffer in the long-term. The other company may be more interested in its perception and reputation, but also sees the bottom line as important. In a military organization it's quite amazing that the culture is almost always determined by the commander and the commander sets the cultural standards and the reputation of the organization. It is somewhat similar in the civilian world. The senior leader sets the example which determines, to a large degree, the culture of the company. If the only thing they are worried about is the bottom line, that will be the prevailing culture. However, if they embrace actions that speak to strong ethical standards, that is what their people will embrace.

This gets us to another point about sharing knowledge. Knowledge is power and as you share it, this augments the health of an organization. Not doing so hinders the organization's success. How should leaders address this?

When you do share that knowledge, you are relinquishing some amount of power. Depending on how it's done, you could be eventually building greater power because you've built a greater consensus base. But, I agree, you have to be willing to share that knowledge and relinquish power. People will see the leader and they will act accordingly. Sometimes people see what a leader has done and they misinterpret it because that leader is not communicating well. He didn't make it clear why he took a certain action or what forces he was dealing with to make a particular decision. So, set the example but also communicate with your people so they know why you did something before it is misinterpreted.

The economic climate we've been in over the last few years combined with rapidly shifting environments is greatly impacting organizations. There is more transparency and we are living in a global business community. How can leaders prepare themselves to face this shifting and rapidly changing environment? What would you say to leaders who are dealing with these kinds of issues?

Well, they've got to stay current with technology for one thing. That doesn't mean you have to be on Twitter or be active on Facebook. But you do have to understand what those things are and what people are doing to communicate and how it can affect your goals and what you want your organization to do and be. So I think you've got to stay technically alert and, to some degree, technically confident yourself. It's not just about technology. It's about how people think. People do think quite differently now than when we were starting our careers in the mid-70's. The world is changing faster and a lot of it is because of the ability to communicate much more rapidly and in so many different ways. But there is an enormous amount of misinformation out there. It's astounding the things that you can read on the Internet that are absolute nonsense. Again applying common sense is very key here. I'm amazed at some of the misinformation out there and how people just assume that it's true. They will take action as a result of this bad information before applying some needed critical thinking.

We all can look back at our lives and realize that we might have done some things differently. We might have prepared ourselves a little differently knowing what we know now. In looking back at your own career, are there some areas where you might have done things differently, possibly different ways you might have prepared yourself or different approaches you might have taken when it comes to your own development or working with people?

I would probably have read more. I didn't read much. I still don't and for me reading is a real time–consumer. I would rather be playing golf or something more pleasurable. But reading is so critical. You don't have to get engulfed in a book everyday but being more broadly informed and well read I think is something that I would probably change in developing my career. I don't have any regrets. I certainly did okay in the Army. But I think I would have been more efficient and more effective if I had read more. I think reading and having a broad knowledge of things is more important than I gave it credit as I 'grew up'

Let me wrap up here. If you were sitting in a classroom of aspiring business leaders and were going to leave them with some critical points of information, what would those key points be? What would you want them to hold on to?

I think the biggest thing is take it seriously because you have enormous influence on people when you are a leader. One of the things that has been actually heartwarming for me but also somewhat surprising goes back to when I was a battalion commander. Many of my lieutenants back then are now colonels and brigadier generals. I run into these guys all the time and they say "I remember the first time that you got us all together", and then they go through these things that I told them. And I say "Man, you guys really were listening".

When you become a battalion commander, you are asked and to write out your command philosophy. Some people would write five single spaced pages as their command philosophy which nobody read. My command philosophy was less than a page double spaced and it started off with, I call it, "golden rule leadership". It was to treat people the way you want to be treated. I had different points that were subordinate to that idea but it was basically to treat people the way you want to be treated. It always amazed me when I was growing up how some leaders would be abusive to their subordinates. I thought "how would he like it if somebody treated him that way". It was just amazing to me that leaders would do that. It's so counterproductive.

A key thought for people seeking to be leaders is to always consider that subordinates will listen to you. They'll watch you and they will remember. You will plant ideas in their heads either how <u>not</u> to do things or how <u>to do</u> things. Rarely is that neutral. You either did it well or you did it badly and they will remember it.

I want to thank you again for your service to the country and for contributing to this important effort. This is candid advice that today's aspiring leaders need to hear.

Kevin, it has been my pleasure.

Chapter 3: Leader Development is Job1

Al Bryant
Former Deputy Task Force Commander for Operation Iraqi Freedom

Meet Al Bryant, Brigadier General (ret) now operating his own management consulting practice. Al currently serves as a program management executive providing executive management and organizational consulting to public-private, private sector, academic, and non-profit entities. He has served as a senior Army Account manager with Booz Allen Hamilton managing service delivery in the areas of program/project and operational effectiveness audit, assessment, and optimization. He advises organizations on matters of expertise, including leadership and diversity initiatives, public-private business development, and multi-disciplinary program management. He served thirty five years in the Army in various leadership capacities to include as the Deputy Commanding General/Assistant Commandant for the United States Army Armor School and the Director of Integration for the United States

25

Army Office of the Deputy Chief of Staff, G-8. He also served as the Assistant Division Commander (Support) for the United States Army 4th Infantry Division (Mechanized), serving as the Principal Deputy to commander of a 30,000 man division task force conducting combat and nation building operations in Iraq in support of Operation Iraqi Freedom.

Al, thanks for being a part of this project. Let's jump right into this. As you know, raising up leaders in any organization is vital for growth. As a senior leader, what do you see as the core responsibilities in raising up our leaders?

First off, let me say that raising leaders is vital for long term health and growth. Let me emphasize the criticality of raising leaders for the health and success of any organization. For any business, organization or institution whose horizon lies beyond the fiscal year or product life cycle, leader development is "Job 1" for every senior leader.

To answer your question directly about core responsibilities, it comes down to the three things. Number one is to ensure that leader development is an intrinsic part of the organization's processes. It is a core capability that the organization must have. An organization that does not expend resources in this area is an organization that will be aimless in a very short period of time and will no longer be able to compete in the environment. The leadership development process should include leader training and education, a formal performance evaluation and promotion system, and a mechanism to identify lateral sources of leaders from outside the core group. In healthy organizations leaders at all levels can be drawn from both within and outside of the organization to ensure access to new ideas and energy. Promoting leaders from within provides continuity and rewards effort and success. It can also lead to cronyism, rigidity of thinking, and the tendency to choose leaders in the same mold as the current leadership. All leaders don't have to come from within the organization. They can be raised elsewhere and brought into the organization. Senior leaders must ensure that the process for leader development is fair, impartial and constantly places the future needs of the organization ahead of personal preferences.

Second, a senior leader serves as a talent evaluator. That is, the senior leader has to regularly look down through the organization and identify those junior leaders with the talents, work ethic, and values needed for success at more senior leadership positions. Assent to leadership positions in most organizations is a limited and therefore, competitive process. So, personally identifying and looking to mentor those types of people or those skill sets and attributes is important.

The third critical responsibility is being able to understand and define the differing leadership skills and attributes required at different levels within any organization. Each organization is different but generally I would identify three different types of leaders commonly found in business, government, and other large organizations.

First, you have direct leadership functions. These are leaders who direct small groups and teams to produce a specific assigned responsibility, be it a product, a process, or a deliverable of some sort. Often these are junior or entry level leadership positions or are associated with specific technical functions. Strong technical expertise, work ethic, inter-personal skills are common to successful leaders at this level. The second leadership echelon is the mid-level managerial leaders responsible for the actual administration/execution of organization's functions. The titles we often associate with leaders at this echelon are program manager, vice-president, or, in the military, field grade officers. They are management, communications, and process oriented.

The senior or strategic leader populates the third level. This is a very different tier of leadership which requires a different set of skills. Too often organizations will place great value on the tactical and management levels but not on the strategic level. As such, when people at this level are promoted to a senior level, they are not always prepared to think broadly, holistically, or strategically. They often relate near term successes with a successful long range strategy. Often it is just the opposite- "pawn grabbing" in chess often leads to failure as key pieces are left out of position and unable to react to other changes on the board. Frequently, without appropriate training and education, junior leaders will rely solely on the processes and leadership skills that were successful for them in the past but are poor fits at the strategic level.

Just as organizations must adapt to changing situations to enjoy continued success senior leaders must recognize that a key element of any leader development program is the responsibility of senior leaders to sort through to find those candidates for senior leadership who are adaptable and visionary to succeed at the strategic level. This is the difference between doers and thinkers and represents the most significant failure of many leadership development programs. Without senior leaders who understand that the leadership requirements are different at each level and that they should manage the leadership selection processes accordingly, organizations will often witness the "Peter Principle". That is, leaders are promoted to their level of failure, placing the organization at risk.

Recent experience reflects the fact that you have people who are happy being individual contributors. They are not looking to be leaders. They enjoy being the architect, the engineer, the subject matter expert. There are others who aspire to be up and mobile in the organization. In focusing on those aspiring leaders, what would you be looking for in a person that would indicate that they might succeed as a leader?

You have doers and you have thinkers. Doers are strong technically. Thinkers have a greater capacity for visualization. Finding someone who reflects a healthy balance between these two types is the key. A doer is strong in producing a product and leading a process team or a small organization. A pure thinker does not require significant near term technical competence. He has higher capacities for thought, visualization, and adaptability which allows him to see beyond the trees, beyond the forest to the ultimate objective. Doing is the environment of the tactical leader and those who are solely inclined to that role are neither suited or competitive for advancement regardless of the level of their technical competence. Thinking is the domain of the strategic senior leader who must clearly focus on guiding the organization through the uncharted circumstances of the future. Managers lie somewhere in the middle, linking those two groups together.

Those aspiring to upward mobility beyond that of a competent doer must bring a more balanced set of skills to the task of leading multiple processes or organizations. Two skill sets would seem to define those who have the greatest potential for advancement - the ability to understand the "big picture" in its component parts and the ability to communicate effectively both down and up the organization.

The ability to translate corporate goals and visions into practical, operational objectives and, in turn, communicate effectively up the corporate hierarchy is vital. This is needed to ensure a productive workforce. It embodies key skills that set aspiring leaders apart from their peers. Minimal technical competence to understand key process requirements, adaptability, and a mind open to change, hard work and a commitment to constant self- improvement, the ability to communicate effectively, and solid people skills including the willingness to listen and delegate authority are key attributes I look for. In the end these people skills may be the most important as at the strategic level, a leader manages people who are empowered to pursue the long term institutional goals that he has established.

When we entered the Army in the 70's, the Army was in collapse. The systems in the Army had failed and the leadership of the Army had begun a process of rebuilding. By the end of the 80s they had succeeded in building what was arguably the finest peacetime Army ever assembled on the planet. The Army that went off to Panama, Desert Storm, and the Balkans had clearly emerged out of the wreckage of Vietnam to rank with the very best in history. Its superb competence was demonstrated in the 4 day rout of the well-equipped, battle tested, 4th largest army in the world, that of Iraq.

What is a compelling lesson, I think, is that the Army was resurrected by strategic and senior leadership leaders who did not follow the traditional path of Army success, that is, through sequential commands of operational units. Gen. Max Thurman, who served as Vice Chief of Staff of the Army, directing much of this renewal process, was a great example of a non-traditional path to success. He never commanded an operational unit beyond a short stint of a few months as a Colonel. Beyond that his major jobs included service as Chief of the Army's Recruiting Command and as Director of Programming Analysis and Evaluation on the Army staff. Nonetheless, he became the architect of Army recovery efforts because he understood processes and how to visualize the interconnectivity of the various aspects of the Army program and how to bring them together as a unified holistic whole from the top down. Many of the other key Army leaders of this period shared this non-operational background, commanding not divisions but institutional commands and directorates. Because their leader development experiences emphasized the holistic thinking about the solutions to problems, they were well prepared to address the institutional issues confronting them as senior, strategic leaders.

31

Now conversely a lot of emphasis was placed on the vision of our training education systems within the Army to produce the sub-strata leaders who had to be the technical subject matter experts. We created and placed great emphasis on bringing people with technical backgrounds. This allowed for this renaissance within the Army which created this outstanding fighting force. In industry I think there is a similar sort of paradigm. Most companies which focus solely on the optimization of production are profitable in the near term. And they promote people from the ranks of those who created the profit. If those people are not capable of thinking beyond that domain, and don't promote people who are able to look at the next big opportunity, then they will not see growth and success long-term.

Where do you see organizations possibly missing the mark when it comes to raising that next generation of leaders?

I keep emphasizing the responsibility of strategic leadership to identify and develop a set of leaders with broad competencies and the ability to think holistically. Organizations miss the mark when they allow leader development to become stove-piped or when leaders do not ensure diversity in leadership development experiences. There can be a tendency for the senior leaders to be guilty of two things. Number one is to link their personal service horizon with that of the organization. By focusing only on the near term issues of "their watch", they can ignore changes in the future operating environment. Therefore, they can eliminate the requirement to develop leaders prepared to deal with that change and do not emphasize it as part of their leader development programs. Critical to an organization's long term success is the ability of its leaders to lead effective adaptation to changes in the environment. If we fail to develop senior leaders who can recognize or accept change, an organization is in danger of becoming rigid and outdated. If leaders cannot visualize both the impacts of changes in the environment and the opportunities they create, an organization will likely be unable to adapt and may become irrelevant. So it is critical that organizations emphasize flexibility and change management as part of their leader development programs.

Every organization has its own culture, has its own ethos. While this can be a strength of any organization, it can also reduce the effectiveness of leader development. Your strategic leadership must be dominated by those who grew up successfully within that ethos and who will naturally be a bit reluctant to vary from it. Successful strategic leadership recognizes, however, the critical responsibility to develop future leaders that are able to think beyond that culture or ethos when the situation demands it. If they do not emphasize it, it will not happen.

A second mistake in leader development I think is to ignore the centrality of diversity. Often we talk about the idea of diversity but diversity demands both diverse types of people as well as diverse leader development experiences. One size will not fit all unless the organization is intent to single course of action regardless of the circumstances. Leader development targeted at developing technical skills is almost, by definition, stove-piped and will produce

33

competent tactical leadership. From the Army perspective, we can take the example of an entry level Infantry Officer who, following infantry centric training, serves within various infantry formations with competence. Without further training and education, his technical expertise will no longer be sufficient when assigned to a combined arms formation or senior staff position far removed from the infantry environment with which he is familiar. The same is true in a company wherein you have an individual who has worked in a specific process or program within a company for a number of years, participating in advanced education or training to develop his specific technical expertise. Such an individual will not be prepared to move beyond his training and experience. Leader development often fails because it is focused on developing skills relevant to the current job or level of responsibility. The best programs emphasize leader development for the responsibilities beyond an individual's current role. You have to place people in positions that will prepare them to move forward.

The old German Army senior leader development model serves as an interesting example of this process. After a rigorous selection process, the most promising officers were assigned to successive and varying staff positions to familiarize themselves with the institutional processes of building, training, equipping, supplying and employing the Army. Periodically they were assigned to troop units for short assignments to familiarize themselves with the practical, technical execution of military tasks by operational units and then returned to the senior level as soon as possible to successively more important positions. Those who failed to measure up were released from the staff for further service with the army in general. It was from the ranks of these officers trained and educated for senior service that the generals and field marshals were selected to lead the war effort. The whole process was designed to develop senior leaders with broad, holistic thinking skills beginning early in their careers through a series of developmental assignments and periodic reviews.

Diversity also means fostering an environment that allows for differing ideas, approaches and ways of thinking about the problem to be encouraged and embraced. To ensure that is part of your process, you have embrace and develop a deep bench of leader candidates drawn from as many sectors within an organization. This means that senior leaders must aggressively reach out and embrace leadership candidates that are not of the normal candidate pool. This is the historical issue with access for minorities, ethnic groups and women. Similarly, companies that are reluctant to bring leadership in laterally from across differing elements of the organization or from the outside run the risk of suppressing original thinking and the ability to adapt.

Sharing knowledge is important for transparency and building effective teams. How do senior leaders ensure that institutional knowledge is effectively shared so that people are not in the dark?

Two things apply here. One is the business of mentorship and the other business is what I would call open architecture leadership. In the past, we tended to make organizations hierarchical. So the position granted you gave you access to information and individuals who would often closely guard that information because that information gave them power and influence. I certainly have seen that in my career both in the military and in the civilian world, where this hoarding of information and guarding it is for positional advantage. So this idea of an open architecture of information in any organization for every job is important. If every job is truly important, then, to the maximum effectiveness of that organization, ensuring information availability and openness in decision is vital. This enables people to understand why they are putting in the efforts that they are being asked to put in. And what the outcome of those efforts need be and where they need to prioritize their work and how they need to think about it. This results in their bringing to the surface additional good ideas through the system to optimize the operation. And everyone has a greater sense of commitment. Contribution always leads to greater quality control.

Again going back to the 80's, the genius of that Army was that it was a bottom-up fed renaissance. It was not a top-down imposed renaissance. It was one based on wide studies across all the disciplines in the Army. And then that moved up into the integrating levels, from which it then moved up to the Department of Army which looked at how you they resourced those decisions. So open architecture is where the leadership shares information to the greatest degree possible.

This can apply to the business community through an effective communications process. What senior leaders are doing in this process is providing information and then providing conduits for which the workers and the leaders can contribute other ideas to further improve processes, further improve the way things are done, and to evaluate the effectiveness of how these ideas have been applied. This is all with the goal of moving the organization forward, improving its process, improving its efficiency, and improving its effectiveness.

I also mentioned mentorship. To apply mentorship, a senior leader must be able to determine who the potential contributors are and who have the skills to pursue the corporate vision. Who has the flexibility of mind to be the next generation leader in your system? Who are the managers who can become senior leaders? Who are tactical leaders who can become managers? Once you identified them, you then can reinforce this process through an active mentorship process. There are two forms of mentorship. One is official or forma where the leader takes the time to interact with his junior leaders in a fashion that will help their understanding of what is trying to be accomplished, where they are going that fosters this growth of ethos which we have talked about earlier. The senior leader shares with them the vision of where they are going.

The other form of mentorship is the informational mentorship role whereby a senior leader can reach out to selected individuals. It can't be general. It's going to be a very limited group of people. It requires the senior leader to be active in reaching down to his more junior people in development.

We are our own worst critics. If you could turn back the clock and maybe change an approach, change a process, change a way you may have approached a problem, what would you have done? How might you have prepared yourself differently?

Let me say first of all, given that the majority of my career as a leader was spent in the military, I was extremely fortunate. I was given the opportunity to experience both formal education and informal training. I was fortunate to have a great diversity of assignments. When I became a General, I was surprised that some of my peers had spent their entire careers essentially doing one thing - serving with and training soldiers. I found most of them totally unprepared for service with the Army staff or within the generating force where most of the general officer billets were located. I had done a multiplicity of jobs from programming, training, unit leadership, institutional leadership, combat developments to budget allocation. So that diversity of opportunity I think put me in very good stead. Having said that, my greatest failure had to do with solicitation of mentorship and, in general, my failure to realize that I had to embrace the leadership upward. Just as much as I wanted and expected them to embrace me down. Personality and pride were factors. I did not develop a good mentorship base until very late in my career. Had I done so earlier, that would have aided in my development as a senior leader. By not having this mentorship earlier, I had to work hard to understand how to translate my work experience into the longer range vision of the force which made me less productive. Clearly had I built those relationships, it would have positioned me for other opportunities. It caused my productivity to be less than it could be and my opportunity to be less than it could be.

The transition from intermediate leader to senior leader causes one to think about what has to change and how you go about doing things. I think that I could have certainly improved my own performance had I spent some significant time studying and reflecting upon what kind of change was needed. So it would have been incumbent upon me to self-study through reading and the seeking out of counsel.

If you were talking to a group of aspiring leaders, and you wanted to leave them with a couple of key thoughts on leadership, what nuggets would you want to leave them with?

The first is that people are the single most important asset that you have. And therefore leadership is the single most important skill that can be brought to an organization. That means that leader development is arguably Job 1 in any organization. Second, leadership comes in many levels and is different in each level. The skills, attributes, and abilities necessary to do each one successfully and optimally are different. Some people will be extremely good at serving as SMEs. But they will not be good at managing and leading people. There are some people that are very good at managing and leading people. We must offer people development processes to bring out their leadership skills. The third thing is that diversity in thinking, diversity in experience, diversity in background are all key contributors to a successful leadership environment. What ties them all together is a common set of values and ethos which the senior leader must promulgate and communicate on a continuous basis through his organization and demonstrate through his own behavior and leadership styles.

Al, thank you for service to the country, for your insights and for participating in this project. Your contribution will bring great value to the business community and to those who are seeking insight and advice on leadership.

Kevin, it was my privilege.

Chapter 4: Never Forget the Soldier, Student, and Client

Bill Campbell
Former Chief Information Officer for the U.S. Army

Meet Bill Campbell, Lieutenant General (ret) now serving as a consultant and military advisor. During his 38-year Army career, Bill served in operations and military intelligence assignments in the United States, Korea, Germany and Vietnam, with command tours from company through brigade. His General Officer assignments included nine years in Program Executive Officer positions and four years in senior staff jobs. His career culminated with duty as the Army's Director of Information Systems for Command, Control, Communications and Computers, Chief Information Officer (CIO) of the US Army, and Military Deputy for C4 systems to the Army Acquisition Executive. After military retirement, Bill worked for the University of California as CIO and Associate Vice President, Information Resources and Communications, with responsibility extending through ten campuses, five medical centers, and three national nuclear laboratories.

Following the terrorist attacks on 9/11/2001, he transitioned to the Defense community as Vice President and General Manager, Information and Communications Networks at BAE Systems, Inc. where he established and led a new business area focused on systems-level solutions for the Nation's war-fighters. He served pro bono on the Army Science Board from 2002 through 2011, was a consultant to the Defense Science Board for two major studies, and co-chaired a National Academy of Sciences study on information technology systems in DOD. He is a past member of the Federal and DOD CIO Councils, DOD's Military Communications and Electronics Board, Microsoft's Global Executive Roundtable, Dell's Platinum Council, the Bay Area Regional Technology Alliance, the National Science Center Advisory Board, and the California Information Technology Commission. He is currently a defense consultant and senior military advisor.

AUTHOR NOTE: I had the privilege of working alongside Bill in his role as chair of the National Academies study committee entitled, "Achieving Effective Acquisition of Information Technology in the Department of Defense". We worked together to assemble a team that included a former Army 4-star, a former Secretary of the Army, and several prominent industry leaders in information technology. He navigated what was a minefield of issues to arrive at a set of recommendations that have served the Defense department well in the modernization of its IT acquisition processes.

Bill, thank you for being a part of this project. Let's jump into this. What I want to start with is a focus on senior leaders raising up leaders. I would like to get your thoughts on what you see as the core responsibilities of that senior leader to raise up the next generation of leaders.

What you just addressed is probably the most important enduring responsibility that senior leaders have. They must set the conditions and foster a culture to develop leadership skills throughout the organization in order to sustain mission readiness today while grooming a cadre of confident and capable leaders for the future. The best organizations I served within the Army, academia, and industry placed a high priority on leader development. It started at the top and permeated the entire organization through education, training, formal mentoring programs, a code of conduct, and a broad range of opportunities for people at all levels to serve in leadership positions. The best senior leaders played a personal role in monitoring succession planning processes and building a bench of potential replacements for all leadership positions to ensure continuity of operations when incumbents depart. They understood that their core responsibilities included passing on down what they learned from their leaders, their mentors, and their experience and encouraging their leadership team to do the same. They set the example in everything they said and did. This is crucial to organizational health because all leadership jobs are transitory. The positions may endure, but all occupants serve for a limited term, and their replacements must be ready to step up and assume higher-level responsibilities

43

on call. One of the strengths of the Army is its bench of highly capable officers and non-commissioned officers ready to assume positions of greater responsibility. Upward mobility is engrained in the culture and emphasized from the top down. Every promotion ceremony includes wording about the "potential for increased responsibility" of the individual being promoted.

In the Army, Values and the Warfighter Ethos are constantly emphasized. This keeps a spotlight on the qualities and character that are the underpinnings of effective leadership and teamwork. Similar paradigms exist in effective civilian organizations. At BAE Systems, Inc. leaders routinely reference their motto, "we protect those who protect us," as a moral compass and a reminder to the workforce that their products serve the warfighter.

Grooming leaders for senior positions is a continuous long term process. It takes more than 20 years to prepare a soldier for selection to General Officer and to prepare industrial leaders for executive level positions (although there are notable exceptions among some high tech entrepreneurs). Raising up the next generation of leaders is a core responsibility shared by all who serve in leadership positions. Their imperative is to develop people with strong moral values and leadership skills who focus on the mission first and people always, whether their ultimate role is on the shop floor or in the executive suite.

There are people who are satisfied being individual contributors. They are not necessarily aspiring to step into leadership positions. I think

organizations are accommodating that now. However, there are also people who do want to be leaders, people who want to step up and to take on those responsibilities. What do you look for in a person who you know is aspiring to be a leader? What are some of the things you like to see in them so that you can have a sense that they would succeed or at least be considered someone who can step into leadership?

The basic attributes I look for in aspiring leaders are character, personal courage, professional competence, and compassion for others. Leadership is an intangible quality. It comes easier to some than others, but there are many examples of great leaders who excelled in spite of a shortage of natural talent. I place a high premium on such characteristics as dedication, capacity to work and learn, perseverance in the face of challenges, ability to build effective relationships, communications skills, a sense of urgency in completing assigned tasks, enthusiasm, confidence, selfless devotion to the team, and physical and moral strengths. These characteristics may be well defined or they may be latent. The key is to be able to assess the candidates' potential to develop leadership skills and to build their confidence through training and experience.

For high level leadership positions, I look for people with vision who can deal with ambiguity decisively, people who can motivate teams to single-mindedly focus on the mission, people with a history of success in challenging jobs, people who put service before self ("careerism" is a disqualifier), and people who are open to coaching and development. I look for

45

those who have a desire to win, learn, stay proficient, and constantly improve. Nobody has all of the attributes I mentioned, but skill sets can be developed and enhanced through, practice, mentoring and experience. It is the job of the leader to recognize and nurture potential, to hone and shape leadership skills, and to mentor high potential leadership candidates. As a leader, I tried to sustain a culture in which members of the workforce understood that over the course of a career they should be prepared to fill multiple roles -- sometimes as a follower, sometimes as a leader, but always a member of a team.

Let me comment further on the individual contributors you mentioned. They play an essential role as members of teams, and even those who profess to be in their comfort zone as individual contributors often play de facto leadership roles (i.e., influencing others). The role of the de jure leader is to motivate, integrate, coordinate and focus the team members on the desired mission or objective. The leader also has a collateral responsibility to help people "be all they can be" and aspire to reach personal goals consistent with their potential, especially those who have the ability but lack the confidence to move beyond their current role.

In that regard, let me mention a personal experience I had not thought about in years until you asked me this question. When I went to college on a football scholarship, I found myself in the lower half of my cohort in terms of size, and I worried about making the team. However, when I entered the gymnasium I saw a plaque dedicated to one of the former coaches that read, "He took them all, big and small, and molded men." That simple quote gave me hope and confidence, and as a result I played football for four years and was ultimately selected as an Academic All American (honorable mention). That experience gave me the personal confidence later in life to step out of my comfort zone and accept challenging responsibilities. When I think in terms of leadership responsibilities today, I see that quote about molding men as relevant in most environments. As an Army officer, I believed I had a responsibility to all my soldiers to help them develop their technical and tactical skills and build their confidence to serve as leaders.

Today's Army has no career privates. No one gets to serve as a soldier for more than a very short period without taking on leadership responsibilities. Lieutenants come into the Army with an inherent responsibility to fill positions of leadership, and most move rapidly up the ranks to captain and beyond; enlisted soldiers come in as privates and quickly advance through the ranks to specialist, corporal or sergeant.

Historically, the Army has had to count on junior soldiers to step up in battlefield situations to replace casualties and take on leadership roles and responsibilities prematurely in the most demanding circumstances imaginable. Some stepped up eagerly, others reluctantly; some excelled, some failed; but in well-trained units, continuity of leadership was sustained. The commercial work place has many similarities. I believe it's crucial for organizations to nurture and sustain a culture that prepares and motivates the workforce to seek greater responsibility and aspire to lead at appropriate levels throughout their careers – individual contributors included.

Having served in senior leadership at multiple levels in the Army and now in the business world, I would like your thoughts on where you see organizations missing the mark, what they may not be doing that they should be doing to raise up leaders effectively.

That's a tough question because I have worked with so many organizations and so many people in the past 50 years. Over that period, I was fortunate to work for successful organizations that I greatly admire. Nonetheless, there were elements of "the good, the bad, and the ugly" present virtually all the time. The Army is a very big, highly dispersed organization, as are the academic and industrial organizations with which I have worked, and they've all had their good and not-so-good times. Consequently, I can't generalize and paint the whole of these large organizations with the same brush.

That said, I believe the two most important practices I observed in organizations that raised up leaders effectively were (1) fostering a "command climate" in which there was mutual respect up, down, and sideways and (2) maintaining effective formal and informal leadership development programs. Where organizations (or organizational units) missed the mark in performance, there was always an element of leadership weakness or failure -- when senior leaders lost the bubble on their organization's internal behavior or when they were blind-sided by external forces that the leadership team didn't anticipate or couldn't handle. In some cases, it took a serious organizational failure to expose a chronic failure in raising up effective leaders over a period of time.

Looking back at organizational units where I worked over my career, I can recall both effective units and dysfunctional units. The biggest difference between these two groups was the quality of leadership from the top down. The effective units had environments where people aspired to become leaders or reliable contributors at all levels. The opposite was true in climates where leaders were distracted, ineffective, or not trusted. Organizations missed the mark when their leadership teams did not deal proactively with their environments (internal and external including customers, competitors, suppliers, and regulators). Causal factors for leadership development failures included the inability to deal with periods of extreme organizational duress; excessive emphasis on near term metrics and quarterly reports; cutthroat competition for promotions; ambiguous or competing organizational objectives; undervaluing teamwork; leaders who were self-servers; and a lack of genuine concern and caring for people in the workforce. When these types of seriously negative conditions existed, it usually took an infusion of new leadership to effect a turn-around. Only then could the conditions be set for raising up the next generation of effective leaders.

I think some organizations create leadership development problems by excessive use of "templates" to define career development patterns for leaders. My thoughts on the effects of templating on leader development were reinforced by an article titled "Solitude and Leadership" that's relevant to this discussion. The article published a lecture given to the plebe class at West Point in October 2009 by Professor William Deresiewicz of Yale University. He said that while Yale, the Military Academy, and other leading universities have a mission to produce national leaders, they are primarily producing conformists and "ticket punchers." He pointed out that templating has become a standard practice in many parts of our society. It's rampant within admissions processes at colleges and universities, and it's prevalent in human resource management. When high school students apply to some of the more selective colleges and universities, they need to have strong academic credentials and 10 or 12 extracurricular and public service activities that, in the end, constitute a punch list. In much the same way, many organizational hiring and promotion practices employ templates or the equivalent. When templates are too rigorously applied over time, people become good at punching tickets – but not necessarily good at strategic thinking, decision-making in the face of ambiguity, or sensing threats and opportunities in their nascent stages. I was jolted by the professor's assertion that the Army has generally not rewarded the capacity to think outside of the box, and that most officers are more conformist than innovative or visionary. This situation is problematic when our Nation needs leaders who are entrepreneurs, innovators, visionaries, prudent risk takers, and change agents who have the capacity to think effectively in a rapidly changing world and reach beyond their grasp (e.g., Steve Jobs). What this means to me is that leadership development programs should include opportunities to study successful strategic leadership use cases and to serve in an "initiative group" or a "skunk works" to get hands-on experience in entrepreneurship and innovation.

Now, I don't mean to say that conforming is bad. Following orders, doing your job, and complying with standards are important. However, when it comes to the question of developing innovative and visionary leaders, some of those who might otherwise have risen to the top lose their way by rigidly following a ticket-punching approach to managing their careers. Consequently, I applaud the Army for its practice of sending selected mid-career leaders to Harvard, Princeton or other universities in lieu of attending one of the war colleges. This type of outreach is a broadening experience that should be included in senior leader development programs. Since I am inclined to believe that the professor is right, I believe that organizations are missing the mark when they do not have a fast-track path for high potential senior leadership candidates that includes spending some quality time in learning environments where they can hone skills in critical thinking.

One important area that I believe a senior leader can greatly impact, even sometimes unconsciously, is the culture of an organization. What would you say to other senior leaders about how they can impact their organization's culture in such a way that it becomes more conducive to the development of future leaders?

You're spot-on about the importance of culture. All organizations have cultures whether documented or undocumented. Everything leaders and decision-makers say and do shapes and drives the de facto culture, with walking-the-walk being more important than talking-the-talk. Senior leaders understand this. They also understand that people respond to incentives, as we all know from Economics 101. What they may not understand in depth is how their organization's culture has evolved and how it is affecting leader development today.

So, in response to your question, what I would tell senior leaders to take stock of both the quality of their current leadership team and their organization's de facto culture as a matter of routine. They should ask themselves whether the bench of emerging leaders has the qualities desired and whether their organization's culture helps or hinders the development of future leaders. I would recommend they take a deep introspective look at how their own actions and policies affect the organization in general and leader development in particular. This includes obtaining feedback on their workforce's perceptions. I think they know intuitively that they set the tone by everything they say and do. But they will need an outside assessment to understand how they are perceived and to recognize their own blind spots. Most organizations have processes to obtain feedback from the workforce (e.g., 360 reviews and externally administered questionnaires or surveys) to support such assessments.

When the leadership team understands the "as is" state of their organizational culture, they can make the adjustments necessary to arrive at the "to be" state. The first critical steps are to codify a clear description of the desired organizational culture, ensure buy-in by organizational leaders, publish it to the workforce, and measure its instantiation on a regular basis. With that as a framework, the leadership team can grow or hire leaders who reflect the values of that culture and act accordingly.

One of the most effective methods to sustain the desired organizational culture is through guidance to boards and decision-makers selecting key leaders and participants in fast-track executive development programs. Such guidance should spell out the characteristics sought in qualified candidates and reflect the values and cultural characteristics envisioned for the organization of the future. Position descriptions should identify those same characteristics. A fast-track program for leader development should include tailored training to hone their leadership skills (e.g., strategic thinking seminars at universities and developmental assignments to broaden perspectives).

Leaders everywhere need to look beyond just the metrics associated with mission accomplishments when evaluating performance. Peer reviews and 360 reviews can provide valuable insights. The best insights into a leader's effectiveness are through the eyes of those who are led. An organization's culture should embrace feedback to identify any toxic people in leadership positions who go beyond healthy aspirations to blind ambition and self-serving actions, which are destructive. They have a negative impact on the organization and teach observers the wrong ways to climb the upward mobility ladder. People learn from what they observe, and when the culture inadvertently promotes self-serving, it conveys a message that each person should take care of number one first.

When you retired from the Army and moved to Academia and then to the business world, did you see any differences in terms of leadership philosophy? Did you see different perspectives or different approaches?

Yes, but the differences are more in degree than kind. There are more commonalities than you might expect, especially at the senior leadership levels. The differences across those three domains are largely in the application and tailoring of leadership approaches to the norms of the organization. To generalize, the military had the most authoritarian philosophy; the academic community practiced the most participative philosophy; and business had the most delegative philosophy. However, I observed all three philosophies in operation at the same time within elements of large organizations. There were different management techniques, leadership approaches, and leadership philosophies in effect at various points along a continuum. I observed that leading and motivating professors in a university and leading the university's administrative staff require different approaches; leading the engineering staff in a high tech firm is different from leading the workforce on the production floor; and leading a battalion of soldiers is different in many ways from leading a military research and development command. What's common is the underlying fact that leaders are dealing with human beings and leadership is all about human skills.

Leadership is still the art of convincing people to accomplish a desired goal, even if it involves hardship or risks. Let me point out here that there are environments within these domains that do not have a counterpart with the other. For example, the Army's combat and basic training environments do not have parallels in the academic and business units where I worked. So my comments relate to leadership in those environments that are common across military, academic, and business organizations.

There were, unfortunately, some toxic leaders in all large organizations where I worked. Fortunately, most were culled out early. Good leaders I observed in industry, academia, and the military had a common base of leadership traits and skills. That wasn't surprising because all three draw both the leaders and the rank-and-file from the same American population. Leaders had similar educational backgrounds, and the workforce had values and expectations that reflected those of American society. Leaders in all three domains were responsible for accomplishing their missions and sustaining their workforce. They had to build relationships, communicate, and take care of the people they were leading.

For the most part, they knew that leadership was more a function of behavior than the position they were filling. The good leaders knew that leadership was more a way of life than a set of tools and that there should be a high degree of mutual ownership in goals and shared values. In all domains, I was pleased to see leaders who had the confidence and the courage to stand up and take the blame and to share or give the credit. They knew that leadership wasn't giving a great speech once per quarter. It was how they behaved every day.

I once heard a civilian leader quote the Buddhist maxim, "You can't pour from an empty cup." What that meant is that you had to fill your own cup with your strengths of character, your feelings of empathy, your tactical and technical proficiency, your physical and mental energy, your personal courage, your caring for others. You couldn't be devoid of those things if you were to build leaders within our organization. I think that description applies to good leaders across the three domains we're discussing.

Here's another similarity. When I joined BAE Systems, the CEO asked me to participate in his leader development program as a mentor. When he asked me about mentoring in the Army, I described a program that began with a discussion of the etymology of the word mentor and went back to the Odyssey written by Homer. There were three main characters: Odysseus, the king, who was going off to fight in the Trojan Wars; his son Telemachus; and his trusted friend, Mentor. When Odysseus went off to war, he knew he would not return for many years. His son would have grown up by then. He realized that he wasn't going to be there to shepherd his son from boyhood into manhood. So he entrusted his son to Mentor. Today the word mentoring carries the deep connotation of Homer's story. Mentoring is about dealing with humans and human behavior, helping people to build their skills and confidence, and getting them started and pointed in the right direction. The CEO said that was exactly what he wanted his mentorship program to be.

Perhaps the biggest difference between military and civilian leadership is that it's easier on the civilian side to reach the top without having gone through every stage of a career development process. You can find CEOs from their 20s and 30s as well as in their 50s or 60s. A special case is in high tech start-ups where some leaders get to the top by being the inventor or a great technician, even if they are jerks. For example, according to his biography, Steve Jobs was a visionary leader who changed the world. However, he was very nasty with people. Nonetheless, he had a team of people who stayed with him and shared his passion. Steve Jobs would not have survived as a leader in the Army, but he was highly successful in the commercial world.

So, in sum, I think leaders in all three domains take the view that leaders are made, not born. Some candidates have more leadership traits than others to build upon, but nobody becomes a leader by just reading a book or being naturally gifted. It is a little bit like pole-vaulting. You can't become a good pole-vaulter by simply reading on how it's done, or watching somebody else. You have to learn the fundamentals and practice hard. And if you stop practicing, you lose your skills. Leadership is the same. It involves giving people responsibilities, providing them guidance, and being there to provide help when needed. Providing leadership candidates the opportunity to lead in a relevant environment is necessary to build their skill sets. Moreover, the transformational leaders and the visionaries of the future need to have time, quiet time, to think. They also need venues where they can meet or surround themselves with the smartest people they can, interact with people who have the most relevant experience, and then iterate the process with increased levels of complexity and responsibility.

Some people, as you know, see knowledge as personal power. Others see it as organizational power. I'd like your thoughts on knowledge sharing and being transparent as it pertains to a healthy organization and the development of junior leaders.

Information sharing is vital. Information is the lifeblood of an organization. It's a dominant element of organizational power, and its value increases the more it's shared. Withholding of information to enhance personal power is a garbage game that leaders should not tolerate. The organizational culture should foster collaboration through information sharing. An organization cannot thrive, and junior leaders cannot mature, if information is concealed for personal power.

The senior leader needs to set the example by communicating information, being as transparent as possible, and establishing trust. Staff meetings, small group meetings, town hall meetings, one-on-one meetings, and publications like newsletters, announcements, and web pages are all methods used by healthy organizations to share information. It's important that information flows up, down, and laterally within organizations. In addition, to stay adequately informed at the top, the leader sometimes needs to create opportunities to get information outside of formal channels. I often told officers selected for battalion command that if they wanted to stay current on organizational health, they should have meetings where they could talk to the spouses. Leaders need to be in touch and need to be trusted. They need to engender and earn respect. Fostering an open exchange of relevant information and discouraging information hoarding will help build a high performance team.

Transparency is equally important, but there is a caveat. It is not always possible to be fully transparent, especially when classified information must be protected and can't be shared with everyone. Corporate merger and acquisition is another example of information that must be close-hold. There are also times when a decision made right now with the best information available is infinitely better than a refined decision made after a lengthy process of gathering all relevant information. There is a balance point that applies in most situations, and one size does not fit all in terms of transparency. The test of your actions, your decisions and your behavior is whether they ultimately lead to success and whether they are validated in the after action reports.

What I am hearing from people at all levels is how rapidly things change. The technology, the way we communicate, the expectations that now exist in terms of responding to situations and so on. I know you have had to deal with this. What tips would you give to leaders today, the younger ones who in fact have more so grown up with this technology than we did? What would you say to them in terms of how to manage all of these new factors that are now impacting how they lead, how they work with people, how they communicate with people?

First, recognize how social media are changing the world, with information traveling faster than ever and rapidly flooding whole organizations. Take time out from your busy schedule to understand how the younger generation employs digital technology and social media as a matter of routine and how to leverage the technology and skill sets in the work environment. If you don't, you may become a dinosaur in the eyes of younger employees.

Today's senior leaders have to recognize these phenomena and have a structure in place to accommodate the new reality. Social media are tools that organizations must use effectively, while taking care to ensure they do not become a distraction. Leaders must recognize that in the digital world virtually everything is recorded and cannot be easily erased. Consequently, one must think before speaking, chose words carefully, and exercise discipline before clicking the send button. The organization must have policies in place for using the full range of communications media. It must be flexible enough to deal with information transmitted outside of traditional channels.

The leader can use the social media infrastructure to disseminate information broadly and rapidly, to track the pulse of what's happening, and to get relevant information to the right audience at the right time. But remember that you risk disenfranchising your staff if you act too quickly with your digital device without allowing the staff officers to do their jobs. Remember, too, that the initial reports and tweets may be wrong, incomplete, or lacking context.

To the younger leaders I would say, resist the temptation to multi-task with your social media device, especially in your work environment; you can't concentrate effectively if you're distracted by reading every text or answering every tweet. Most importantly, silence or shut down your "crackberry" when in meetings or discussions with the boss.

Allow me to get personal. We are our own worst critics. We can look back and see what we might have done differently. If you could turn the clock back, would there be anything you might have prepared yourself differently for? Anything that you might have done somewhat differently in terms of problem solving or how you communicated? Any things you might have changed in terms of how you would have approached an issue?

I would try to be a better listener, read more professional literature, and delegate more. When time permitted, I would seek more counsel and viewpoints before making hard or controversial decisions. I would spend more time engaging with the workforce to sense the organizational climate, answer questions, and receive feedback and recommendations. Throughout my career, I was continually on a steep learning curve. Over my 38 years on active duty, I never got the job I listed on my assignment preference statement. I was initially unprepared in many respects for most jobs I had in the Army, academia, and industry. This led me to surround myself with the smartest people I could find. Looking back, I can recall times when I could have done a better job in giving those people the credit for organizational success.

Last question. Imagine that you are talking with a group of leaders at multiple levels, multiple parts of the business world or even within the military and you are about to leave them. You want

to leave them with some lasting thoughts. What would they be?

With a military audience I would say, never forget the soldier and the impact that your decisions have on him or her. With an academic audience I would say, never forget the students; give them the foundational knowledge necessary to succeed in life and their careers. With an industrial audience I would say, always strive to thrill your customers with your product or service and set a goal to make the "100 best places to work" list.

Bill, are there any personal things you still want to do? Swim the English Channel? Visit certain parts of the world? Anything you still haven't done that you would like to do?

What I would like to do is to stay relevant for as long as possible. I see some people who are my age and younger going out to pasture and losing the opportunity to make important contributions. I don't want to lose such opportunities. I'm not out to change the world, but I would like to continue having a positive effect on the lives of others whether they are friends, business associates, family members, or people of any affiliated group. I find the work environment to be mentally stimulating. Working as a defense consultant lets me stay engaged in a meaningful way following retirement from full time work. I still get a lot of satisfaction when a colleague or a client says, "I have this problem. What did you do in similar circumstances? How did you solve this? Could you help us in reviewing some technology?" That said, I also want balance in my life. I do not have a bucket list, but I would like to travel more with my wife.

Helping others in a professional environment is a part of what I do, but my most important job is being the best husband, parent, and grandparent that I can be.

Bill, thank you for your service to our country and for contributing to this project. Your contribution will bring tremendous value to the business and military leadership communities.

Kevin, it was my pleasure.

Chapter 5: We Are In This Thing Together

Jim Coggin
Former Commanding General
2nd Infantry Division, U.S. Army

Meet Jim Coggin, Major General (ret) now serving as an executive in the IT sector of the defense industry. Jim joined General Dynamics Information Technology's Army Solutions Division as Vice President and General Manager of the Simulations, Training and Instrumentation Solutions sector in September of 2008. In this capacity, he is responsible for the financial and management oversight of business that provides information technology and program support to the U.S. Army and other federal and state governmental agencies. Prior to joining General Dynamics Information Technology, Jim served as the Deputy Business Group General Manager and Mission Systems Group Vice President for Business Operations at CACI, International. In this capacity, he was responsible for the broad direction and oversight of business operations in support of a $750 million dollar business group's objectives, assisting the Business Group General Manager and leadership team in developing and driving the strategic direction for the group and bringing resources to bear for project execution. Prior to CACI, International, he served in the Army for 34 years, retiring as a Major General in 2008. During his career, Jim held a variety of command positions in Panama, Germany, Korea and the U.S. in Infantry units. He commanded the 2nd Infantry Division in Korea, where during armistice and wartime conditions, he was responsible for leading, training, maintaining, caring and overseeing the safe operations for nearly 15,000 assigned and associated support personnel in support of the defense of the Republic of Korea. Jim graduated from the United States Military Academy at West Point with a Bachelor of Science Degree and the Georgia Institute of Technology with a Master of Science Degree in Operations Research. He completed a postgraduate research fellowship with the RAND Corporation in Santa Monica, California.

Jim, thanks very much for being a part of this project. Let's jump right in on this. One vital task of any organization is to raise up and develop leaders. As a senior leader, what do you see as the core responsibilities for a senior leader to make that happen?

I have seen those core responsibilities not only in my 34-year commissioned career within the Army but also in the last 5 years as an executive with General Dynamics. I believe it begins with you as a senior leader modeling the desired goal or behavior that you would like to see of everyone on your team. For example, that means that whatever you ask anyone else to do, you should be doing it as well. If you ask your strategic planner to develop a strategic vision for the future, you should be doing that in parallel. This will equip you to communicate how the vision is going to ultimately come into focus. As you are dealing with the priorities of your organization, you have a role in designing those priorities and focusing action, directing action to achieve your organization goals. You have to think strategically and you have to focus on your priorities and you have to direct action to achieve those goals. Then you have to hold, not only your team accountable for achieving those goals, but you also have to hold yourself accountable. You cannot say that it is someone else's fault. If you are that division commander or you are that vice president and general manager, literally the buck stops with you and you must assume that accountability.

Secondly, I would say that it's incumbent upon that senior leader to build an effective team. There is a great book that has been out for some time now called 'From Good to Great', written by Jim Collins. He offers an analogy related to 'Great Organizations' whereby the senior leader ensures that the right people are on the bus. The bus is a metaphor for the organization. In this metaphor he speaks of the fact that the wrong people need to be off the bus or are out of that organization. And that within that bus or that organization, everyone on the bus sits in the right seat. A senior leader has a core responsibility to make these difficult decisions by assessing those leaders in your organization as to their abilities, motivation, and talent; to evaluate their work ethic and correct them if they are not properly focused; and, if necessary, get them off of the bus and to find the right person to fill that vacant seat.

Senior leaders also have the role of an encourager. You need to be a 'glass half full' type of person. You need to come in everyday positive about your circumstances, independent of the challenges you face. You know that you are going to move forward and you are going to be successful. That is infectious. People want to work around leaders who have a positive outlook.

As senior leaders seek to raise up a person or individual, what attributes do you look for that you believe will be important for them to succeed as a leader?

For me, it begins with a person who is a very hard worker. Someone who does not shy away from the difficult tasks that have to be done. But, more than that, someone who can work in a very collaborative way within a workplace environment. That is very effective. I am also looking for a hardworking team player that possesses professional goals for themselves but equally places full dedication toward the success of the overall team's efforts.

Secondly, I look for an individual that has the potential for senior leader development to be one who really thrives on challenges. They accept the challenge of a difficult job. In my own life, I have found that the most satisfaction that I have had professionally is, when given the opportunity to do very difficult and challenging jobs, to persevere through all the challenges and arrive at the point of success; success not just for yourself personally, but success for the organization. Lastly, I would say that learning is a lifetime endeavor. So I look for someone who is constantly striving for professional development as well as seeking ways to experientially develop opportunities for the group. You are always going to learn new skills and your knowledge base will always be extending. Here in General Dynamics the environment of technology is constantly evolving. To stay in the present is to lose touch with the market. So you must always be seeking to develop yourself and seeking innovative approaches to solving complex problems.

Sometimes organizations may be missing the mark in their efforts to raise up this next generation leaders. What are your thoughts about how organizations might be missing the mark?

It begins with notion of being intentional and being purposeful. I will just identify 2 or 3 points that illustrate some failures that an organization may experience. In some instances they fail to challenge young, high performers who have the potential to grow into senior leadership by not giving them the increased responsibility that, frankly, they would like to have. I think it is incumbent upon all organizations to provide those opportunities. It's the condition within which the young performer will demonstrate that potential and I think we sometimes fall short of that.

Secondly, organizationally in the workplace environment, we fall short sometimes of taking opportunities to be an encourager. Mentorship is used a lot today and I think it's the encourager component that is vital. It is a nurturing function and sometimes organizations fail to do that effectively. On the flipside of all that, if you are a high performing, high potential type of person and you see others who are not performing well and not being held accountable for their less than desirable performance, that high level performer can become discouraged or even disgruntled. You might even lose them which is a greater loss to the organization.

You touched on the environment saying that a poor culture, poor environment can hinder leadership development. How can an organization or its senior leaders ensure that the culture is contributing effectively to leaders emerging effectively?

The current senior leadership must set the conditions in the workplace environment for the nurturing of future senior leaders. What is important is ensuring and enforcing an ethical environment, where integrity and values are being demonstrated every day. A model by which leadership at all levels reflects ethical conduct and how to go about it in the daily workplace environment, providing products and services to customers. Ensuring an ethical workplace environment is absolutely fundamental. And within that environment, those who fall short, those who make a conscious decision to reject those ethical standards and conduct themselves in a way that is detrimental to the workplace environment are held accountable. When I came out of on the brigade commander list, I was looking hopefully at taking command of the second brigade of the 82nd Airborne division. But when the Aberdeen training scandal hit the Army, I was thrust into the largest training group brigade in the Army to address what was a huge organizational failure. Holding accountable those who failed to uphold ethical standards is absolutely fundamental. If you are in any organization where that expectation is not the norm, then you're not going to nurture any leadership, be it senior or junior.

And lastly, I think it's incumbent upon today's leadership to grow tomorrow's leaders. There are all kinds of opportunities for complex and challenging work to be done. Investing in the professional development of high performers is a very effective way for an organization to ensure that they develop properly.

There are some leaders that hold information close and do not share it. And, of course, there are those who do share what they know. Some senior leaders feel a need to control institutional knowledge. What are your thoughts about how leaders should effectively share information and institutional knowledge with their teams and emerging leaders?

I think again it begins with the environment that exists in the organization. What I referred to earlier as a genuine collaborative work place environment applies here. It provides an environment within which everyone's ideas are valued and can serve as a contribution. We've all been places where we see a problem, we bring forth an idea, but no one in the organization is sharing your idea, or encouraging others to share their ideas. This is not healthy. A collaborative work place environment today will ensure that everyone is operating on the same grid. This is incredibly effective and it's a condition within which you will identify those high potential or high performers and put them in the right place where they can really be effective and grow.

And while you are doing that, it's important to take the opportunity to recognize them, to give them rewards. There are all types of programs, whether they are pay increases or bonuses or stock option programs. That's an important job that I have today, taking limited incentive resources and recognizing those deserving of rewards.   That's   very   important.   This   also   rewards innovation where efficiency and effectiveness are prime attributes.

I   mentioned   earlier   about   giving   this   high performance   individual   the   opportunity   to   accept increased challenges. I had three such situations over the last five years. I sought out someone for an entry level position that I thought would be over-qualified within a couple of years for that job. I would put them in that position to give them an increased responsibility over time and then find them a job that is a more functionally focused area where they can grow.

We   work   in   a   rapidly   shifting   business environment wherein we face both economic and technological challenges.   How can leaders better prepare themselves for this kind of rapidly shifting environment?

The economic environment today nationally is challenging. You have to be good stewards of your resources. Current senior leaders must demonstrate due diligence for those emerging leaders who are watching how those resources are being managed and utilized. This   includes   how   you   hire   and   bring   on   new employees. It's not a casual thing. You must do your homework. You must make sure that what you see in that new person validates the attributes and the skills that you are looking for. You don't want to disadvantage the organization with an under performer. You want to ensure that you are actually strengthening your organization. You can only do that at every opportunity you have when you select the truly best available candidate.

Secondly, you must be really careful about decisions pertaining to budgets and expenses. If you don't manage your costs effectively, that's a big problem which can lead to an end of the year failure. The last thing I would say is you have to constantly be scanning the strategic planning horizon. I think one of the key skills for a current senior leader and emerging senior leaders is the ability to anticipate, adapt, and then take action. That comes about by constantly refreshing yourself on market dynamics in the business industry or operational environment within which you serve in uniform. You really need to not only understand where you are now but also where you expect to be in the future. That's really important. There is a book entitled 'Who Moved My Cheese'. The message within it speaks to the point that you need to anticipate when the environment within which you are functioning well may change. You must constantly anticipate and take action to adapt to the changing market or organizational dynamics.

We are all driven to do well we and we can be our own worst critics. If you could turn the clock back and look at what you might have changed,

maybe how you might have approached an issue or how you might have prepared yourself, would there be anything that you would have changed?

Through your career you come to value over time the increasing importance of good relationships and how important they are to an organization's success. I am talking about the human dimension here, how one relates with those with whom you serve with in uniform over time and in the corporate world. It's important to maintain those connections and staying in touch both with friends and professional acquaintances. One might assume that I am focusing on how important these relationships are to furthering one's career. That's not really what I am talking about here. What I'm talking about are genuine, heartfelt relationships with others that you have known and served with. Over time it enriches your life. I think that's something that I could have done more effectively in uniform and it is something that I'm trying to do more effectively in the corporate side of my life. It has to be intentional. You must be purposeful to do it and it takes time. And the struggle I have is the time dimension. It takes time to maintain those relationships.

Secondly, trusting and relying upon your education, training, experiences and, most importantly, the instincts and intuitions that you develop over time. These instincts and intuition don't come from us. They come from the faith that we have in the spiritual dimension frankly. There is a human tendency to defer very hard to decisions to the last possible moment. In my life I can look back and see some hard decisions, whether it was having to remove somebody from a leadership position or make a significant change organizationally, those are hard decisions and I think you just need to make the thoughtful decision required, then take action and get it done diligently. I struggle with that even today.

And then lastly, I would say giving yourself permission or freedom to ask to do harder things. It's easier to get comfortable with what you are doing particularly if you are doing it really well. And I think over my military career there were things that I gained a reputation for doing well and I was asked to do more of the same. I think sometimes it would do us all well to push out and pursue doing the harder things. I would have done more of that.

Let me wind up with this final question. Picture a group of hungry leaders at multiple levels that are gathered around you and you want them to walk away with something that sticks in their minds after you are long gone. What would that be?

First, know the values of your organization. These are foundational. Never compromise on them. We are going to hold each other accountable and I am holding myself accountable. You have my permission to hold me accountable. If I have a blindspot, you have my permission to speak up. That is what we stand upon. In the business world you find different values sometimes but they are brilliant and elegant. They include trust, teamwork, integrity, customer satisfaction and business success. And I would say first and foremost is that developing a nurturing, collaborative cooperative culture is job one.

Secondly, there is an accountability that's applied 24/7. We have to set that example. We know and everyone surrounding us inherently knows what right looks like. We need to live our lives accordingly. There is always going to be the cynic on the sideline who is not in the arena but who is going to judge us. We don't want to necessarily concern ourselves with the cynic on the sideline. But we don't want to give that cynic a basis for his cynicism. So I think holding ourselves to high standards and holding ourselves accountable as we hold each other accountable is really important.

Perhaps the last thing I would say is we are in this thing together. We are going to care for each other. We are going to be concerned about each other. We need to be there for encouragement. We need to be supportive. We care about each other as much as we care about the organization.

Jim, thank you for your service to our country and to this effort. Your insights will provide great value to those who are in leadership roles. I expect it will bring much impact.

Kevin, thanks for the opportunity to contribute.

Chapter 6: Communication is Never Done

David Fastabend
Former Director of Strategy,
Plans, & Policy for the U.S. Army

Meet David Fastabend, Major General, US Army (ret), now a senior industry executive in the cyber world. David is the Vice President of Advanced Information Systems at ITT Exelis. Appointed to this position in January 2011, David is responsible for all aspects of the Advanced Information Systems business area including performance, strategy, leadership, and customer relations. In this capacity he leads the information and cyber solutions strategy to enhance national security by providing information-enabled solutions for federal customers across DoD, intelligence, and civil agencies. Previously, David served as Director of Strategic Planning and Technology Development for Exelis, where he was responsible for shaping the business into a market-centric, customer-focused organization by leading strategic planning efforts.

Prior to joining Exelis, David held a number of leadership positions within the United States Army. In his final assignment as a General Officer, he served as Director of Strategy, Plans and Policy. Prior to that, he served in Iraq as Director of Strategic Operations, Multinational Forces Iraq.

David holds a Master of Military Arts and Sciences degree from the Command and General Staff College, a Master of Science in structural dynamics from the Massachusetts Institute of Technology and a Bachelor of Science from the United States Military Academy. He is a published author and a registered professional engineer in the State of Virginia.

David, thank you for being a part of this project. Let's jump right in. Given the importance for senior leaders to raise up the next generation of leadership within an organization, what do you see as the core responsibilities as a senior leader in raising up new leaders?

Well, I think in any organization you have to embrace the reality that new leaders drive the organization forward. Typically it is new leaders who are actually leading performance at the cutting edge: at the mid-tier and at lower-tier levels of the organization. So if you have an organization that wants to perform now and you look at where it's performing best and who is contributing most to it, you begin to understand who those people are. In my experience, it would be highly unusual to find that the people who are going to be the future leaders of the organization would be an entirely different set of people -- they are in fact these very people who populate the organization at the cutting edge. You can certainly complement them by bringing in outside talent at certain points, but I think there's a close linkage between leading an organization in its current mission and at the same time preparing it for its future one.

Experience is now showing that there are people who aspire to be leaders, looking to step up into those responsibilities. And then you have those who are happy to serve as technical contributors, subject matter experts, not necessarily wanting to be in a leadership role. As you look within an organization, trying to identify people who could succeed as a leader, what would you be looking for in a person to succeed in this capacity?

Well you definitely have to look for someone who has a large and well established degree of technical understanding. No matter what profession you are in, a technical understanding is always important. And you want people that are able to execute at their current level of responsibilities. If someone routinely fails at their current level, it's highly improbable that promoting them is going to solve the execution problem. But I also have come to believe that a senior leader needs a high degree of emotional intelligence. I don't know if I could define it but I think everyone understands what emotional intelligence is. And although people need it really early in life, I think it's less important at a junior level, frankly. Proportionally it becomes more important as people rise up in the ranks. Typically, when you find someone who is performing well at a certain level but seems to falter at the next level, in my experience, this can be traced to some challenge with or lack of emotional intelligence. The techniques they were using or the relationships they had developed at a certain level didn't migrate very well to the next. So I believe it is vital to examine folks to see how they are doing in the emotional intelligence dimension. That's a big flag for me.

I worked on a project recently where that was a big issue. There were people who were actually in management or in a senior position who had blindspots in that area. It was causing some issues within the organization. And to the organization's credit, they were trying to resolve that. This runs into another point, however. Sometimes organizations can miss the mark in addressing these types of issues. Sometimes they simply have blindspots and are not aware of what they need to be doing when it comes to leadership development. In your view, where do you see organizations missing the mark and what should they be doing in this area?

Well, I'll talk about something that, frankly, I'm still wrestling with. One of the pleasures of working in industry after working in the government is that there is a level of accountability in industry that people in the government don't really appreciate or understand until they experience it. Now don't get me wrong. I know there is what we in the Army used to call the "contract of unlimited liability". Certainly there are very important notions of ethical, moral, and leadership accountability in the military. But there's a level of fiscal accountability in industry that is amazingly pervasive. It drives an organization's competiveness in a market. I mention that because in the government, at least in the military, we invested heavily in leadership development programs. But the cost of those programs was transparent to us. A large percentage of our military careers were devoted simply to training. I think it varied between 25% to 30% of my career being in some kind of academic, training, or educational experience. Industry organizations simply can't afford that. Even very simple training requirements and certifications for training requirements are sometimes financially out of reach. Every time such an opportunity arises for training, the challenge is determining how to handle that expense. How do I charge that?

So you have to address those tradeoffs immediately in industry. Those tradeoffs existed in government but they were totally invisible to you. You just went to Command General Staff College for a year. Then you stayed an extra year for the school of Advanced Military Studies because they asked you to and you could. And it prepared you for your mission. So one of the biggest challenges in industry in developing leaders is balancing the natural tension between the investment and the time you devote to it, along with the use of these people to execute your business mission. To me, that is the fundamental conundrum at the heart of how to deal with a lot of the leader development challenges in industry. Our company does it. I have a training budget.

You're speaking to cultural issues very specifically in drawing those comparisons between your experience in government and the military and civilian life. What thoughts might you have about how a leader can impact the culture in such a way

81

that the culture becomes an enabler to help these leaders emerge effectively?

I was once actually assigned a major Army project about the Army's "culture." So I've had a chance to think about culture a bit. The project put me in charge of a task force, the mission of which was to instill a culture of a "joint and expeditionary mindset" in the Army. So we went into some fairly philosophical discussions: "What is culture" and "How do you influence it?" I'll spare you the days of discussion about these questions. But I came away from it convinced about a handful of things regarding culture. First of all, it's very difficult to define a culture because culture almost by definition is made up of the things you do or think 'automatically', without even realizing its part of your culture. If you can articulate "I'm doing this because it's my culture", that's probably not really your culture. It's probably a reason or an idea you have - culture is more innate and intuitive.

We also determined that if you want to instill a joint and expeditionary mindset in the Army, then you need to consistently, routinely, and frequently <u>do</u> joint and expeditionary things. In other words the culture doesn't drive the behavior. The behavior eventually drives the culture. Cultures develop after long periods of routine, repeated behavior. So when I think about culture in any organization and how I want to change it, I start thinking about the behaviors that we want to instill and we start trying to demonstrate them. For instance, I'd like to improve a culture of communication in my business right now. I get a lot of input that people don't communicate with each other. I'm not going to run to people and say "hey, communicate more". I'm just going to start communicating more myself. And that's what I try to do. I try to communicate using as many techniques as I can find: email, townhall meetings, visits, one-on–one discussions. I also have a blog. I do all of that stuff just to demonstrate by example the cultural behaviors I want people to adopt.

You know I am glad you brought those last points up. Previously, I participated on a contract with the Army addressing the very difficult topic of sexual harassment and assault in the Army. General Casey had contracted with our organization to come in and train senior non-commissioned officers and company grade officers in this area. It was very eye opening to see the cultural divide between the senior and junior levels of the Army on this issue and how it was viewed. In working to impact the culture in this area, the issue of sharing knowledge effectively emerged as a critical issue. Some see knowledge as power and, as such, may not be as forthright in sharing it. What are your thoughts about this whole idea of how to use and effectively share institutional knowledge and how can a senior leader effectively contribute to that process so that emerging leaders are being properly equipped?

I don't think anyone wakes up and says "I know some things and I'm not going to let someone else know". I just don't think they do. We live and work in such a connected world today that doing your job alone is non-sensical. I have 1600 people in my organization. I can't do anything without many other people either knowing or being involved in some way, directly or indirectly. Many people don't share information very effectively. But it's only because they haven't mastered the art of dealing with the amount of knowledge they have to process.

It's impossible to process everything that is flowing toward and through you. You cannot schedule your life wall-to-wall and do nothing but attend meetings, particularly if those meetings are nothing but input to you. If all you do is attend meetings, you are not giving yourself time to process what you have found out. So I consider a day where I am scheduled wall-to-wall a disaster. I try to react to it and fix it because I know I'll do nothing but get input. I will be handed problems. I may have a random thought that I'll jot down during the meeting. But I will not have time to take all that insight and process it into useful knowledge for others. So there has to be a balance between what you're taking in and what you put out.

Now I have some other techniques I use. I take notes by hand in my meetings typically. Sometime during the day I transcribe my notes into a Word file. Some people write in these green books. I have always admired these people who do so, but my handwriting is not that neat and organized. So I will make my notes on briefing slides and all sorts of pieces of paper. But at some point within a few days of those meetings, I will transcribe those notes and, in that transcription, I will actually organize my thoughts about them. I've been doing this for years. I maintain an outline of my notes, annotated day by day, meeting by meeting. I frequently will go back to those notes. Just the thought of synthesizing them has been very useful to me to process all that input and to turn it into knowledge.

But your obligation as a leader is to communicate it. For example, I just came back from a leadership conference. If I don't transmit that knowledge to my subordinates and what I got out of that conference, I have wasted the time I spent attending it. That conference was not for my personal and professional development. It's for the organization and I've got to somehow be able to synthesize what came out of there and send it back down appropriately to my organization.

Technological advances and economic challenges are causing significant shifts to the business environment. How do you think leaders can prepare themselves to adjust to these changes as they lead their organizations?

You must be open to using the technology tools as they present themselves to you. Imagine what life would be like for you or me if, the first time, we were presented with a computer we said "No, I like doing my stuff on a typewriter". Or the first time someone wanted to give us a laptop, I said "No, I like my desktop because I know where it is and it's connected to the printer. I don't want to carry this thing around." Or first time you saw the opportunity of an iPhone, you said "Wow, I don't want to have to type things on my phone. Phones are just for talking." Most of us are used to the fact that technology is going to change on us. You've got to realize it's going to come and the tool you're really fond of is going to be obsolete in a few years. It's amazing to me how much it's evolved when you think about it. I didn't have a desktop until I went to Command & General Staff College. I was a major. That was 1985. Now you get a new device. You don't get an instruction manual anymore. You turn it on and figure it out and if you can't, you go on the web somewhere and people tell you. You somehow figure it out. And so I think as far the new tools are concerned, you have to have an open mind. I think most of us have that. I also think you have to have the ability to do some critical reasoning because some of the stuff that comes at you will be overblown, in my opinion. You have to be cautious about how you approach it. Some things will come at you with a lot of hype. But when you get into it and peel the covers back, you find that as far as being applicable to your business, it's a challenge.

I'll say one more thing about the impact of technology on leadership. Most of this technology is message technology. If you send something to someone and you assume the communication task is done because they are going to read it, you should not be too confident that you have successfully communicated. There is still a huge role for relationships and for phone calls and for face-to-face conversations. And that's one of the things I am still challenged by. I do a lot of email communication because it's the only way I can technically reach a workforce that is all across the country and overseas. It's the only way I can get to them. But I don't feel like I'm in touch with them necessarily because it's very hard to get to them physically. At times you need to do go see them. And I think leaders need to understand that technology is not going to solve the problem of establishing a relationship with your workforce. You have to work hard at that because people will fall back to some of these other methods of communicating, which have their place. But they cannot replace the relationships.

Let's pose a reflective question. We are all our own worst critics. We tend to do that to ourselves as human beings. If you could turn back the clock and make some changes on how you might have prepared yourself for something in the past, maybe how you might have approached something, would there be any changes you might have made?

Well I think in order to identify regrets, you've got to start with what you wish you were now that you're not so much. A lot of people laugh when I tell them that I am an introvert. I'm the famous joke about the extroverted engineer who looks at the other guy's shoes when he's talking to him. Let me operationalize this for you. When I go to a party, I am not one of those people that within 20 minutes can talk to everyone in the room. I just cannot do that. I don't want to do that. If I latch onto one person who engages me in an interesting conversation for the whole night, I consider that function a huge success. However that's not good in business. I firmly believe in the importance of relationships and I'm big about having relationships. I would like to understand what it was in my upbringing that made me so introverted. I would then go back and fix that. It's just the way I am. And I think it's one of those conditions. We all have them. I have to accept it. You try to compensate for it. That's my main regret: that I ended up so introverted.

Let me roll down to this last point which is this: If you were among some aspiring leaders and you wanted to leave them with some thoughts of what not to forget in their role as a leader, what would you share with them?

If I had to condense it down to just a handful of things, I would start out with the relationship part. I would tell people that if you have a relationship with someone, you can solve any problem. If you don't have a relationship with them, everything is a problem. I would tell them that communication is a job that is never done. No matter how well you think you are doing it, you never can do it enough and you have to keep pouring on the effort and the communication. I think it's important for people to understand that people around you will believe that what you are thinking about is in fact what you're talking about. You can have very good thoughts but if you only talk about other things, those thoughts are never available to your audience. So often in our dealings with other people, we only talk about what we are worried about, even though there are other things in our mind that are equally important. You might go before an audience that you care about. You are worried about their future and how the business environment is going to impact them. But if you get up there and only talk about your numbers, their conclusion is that you are only thinking about the numbers. So I think that's important.

David, thanks again for our service to our country and for being a part of this project. Your insight will go a long way in bringing value to this discussion on leadership development.

Kevin, thanks for inviting me to be a part.

Chapter 7: Make Leadership Development a Priority, Not Just Lip Service

Steve Hashem
Former Director of Coalition Coordination
US Central Command

Meet Steve Hashem, Major General (ret) now serving as an executive in the defense aerospace industry. Steve is currently with Lockheed Martin Corporation. He is a senior consultant who provides high level marketing guidance and strategy development for the information systems and government solutions and global logistics and training business areas. His career with Lockheed Martin spans 26 years in various assignments with increasing responsibility, to include program operations and business development. His 37 year military career culminated with duty as Director of Coalition Coordination with the United States Central Command. He was responsible for coordinating international support to coalition operations in Iraq and Afghanistan. He worked closely with personnel from

91

over 60 nations. His academic credentials include a BS from West Point in General Engineering, an MBA with a concentration in strategic planning from the Wharton School of Business and an MA from the University of Pennsylvania in International Relations.

Steve, thanks for being a part of this research effort. Leadership is a hot button and an important issue in any organization. Let's start with the topic of raising up leaders. This is vital in any organization. It's vital for the organization to grow, to meet its mission. As a senior leader, what do you see as the core responsibilities for making this happen, for raising up leadership?

It starts with the senior person or leader in an organization. That individual has to set the tone. Developing leaders and leadership training has to be important to him or her. It has to be a part of the culture of that organization. Senior leaders need to create forums or organizations to facilitate leadership development, not just for high potential people, but for as many individuals in the organization as possible. There is a series of steps involved in leadership development. You need to create the criteria for identifying and selecting who your high potential people are. There needs to be training. Individuals also need to be assigned to a variety of positions that are diverse with increasing levels of responsibility. In addition, there needs to be continuous re-evaluation and assessment. Finally, each individual also needs to be provided with feedback and assigned senior mentors.

You made a reference to the need for organizations to focus not just on high potential

leaders, but everyone else as well. What would you be looking for in an individual to identify them as a high potential leader?

It obviously depends on what level and type of leadership we're talking about. There are differences between junior, mid-level and senior leaders, technical and functional leadership as well as leaders who only have pure management responsibilities. Regardless of the type and level of leader we're talking about, I think there are certain attributes that are essential. Leaders need to set the example. They need to have talent and work hard. They need to be visible, have integrity, and also have care and concern for their employees. There are other qualities, but those traits are important for any leader to be effective. In general, I would say that strong character and a high level of competence are the two most important attributes. Many senior leaders often times forget the lessons that they learned as a junior leader and what is really required for effective leadership.

Given your experience, where are organizations missing the mark, what blindspots do organizations have when it comes to raising up leaders?

I would say again that it starts at the top. If senior people don't set the example, if they don't stress the importance of leadership and leadership development and continuous training in their actions and mentoring, it's not going to happen. Unfortunately, leaders tend to focus on short term goals versus long term goals -- financial profits in the short term as

93

opposed to what's best for the organization over the long term. That can affect the way a leader leads and does his or her job. I also think that organizations need to allow people to make mistakes. The way to learn and improve is by doing and that often times entails making mistakes. There are very few mistakes that an organization or individual can't recover from. Organizations need to be more tolerant of people making mistakes. That's how individuals learn and develop as professionals and as leaders.

As you look at culture in an organization, what can senior leaders do to make their culture serve as an enabler to help these new leaders emerge effectively?

Leaders need to avoid the "zero defects" mentality and allow people to make mistakes. I think you've heard of "MBWA", that is, "Management by Walking Around". Senior leaders need to be visible. They need to be engaged. They need to work with people and understand what's going on throughout the organization and especially at the grassroots level. They need to help high potential leaders manage their careers, to make sure that they get the right assignments, the right experience, and the right training. They need to ensure that right incentives are in place. People are going to do what they get measured on and are rewarded for. So, if you're not rewarding them on the right things, you may actually be hindering their development and impacting the success of the organization.

We hear all the time that knowledge is power and that statement can be good or bad depending on how people view and use knowledge. Some people

keep knowledge close to themselves. By not sharing, it they can control others as well as be in control. Senior leaders need to be focused on making sure that people are contributing to the institutional knowledge, developing it and sharing it. So I'd be interested in your thoughts on how a senior leader can enable that to happen and therefore ensure that these new leaders are being properly equipped.

In all of the positions that I have ever been in, either in the military or in the corporate world, I've always made it a point to develop my subordinates and to work with them and to make sure that they have the skills necessary to do -- not only their job -- but my job as well. When you take that approach, it has a couple of benefits. Number one, it benefits the individuals that you're training because they feel that you care about their development. Secondly, it's good for the organization because you never know when a key person may leave or get promoted, thus creating a need for someone to step in and fill that responsibility. I've seen a lot of cases where that mentorship doesn't always occur because the senior leader views the junior person as a threat to his job, which is really the wrong way of looking at it. He should see that individual's development as an asset to the organization.

Speaking of junior leaders, one very evident factor is that the environment technologically has shifted. Today, you've got the ability to communicate in real time. Many businesses are facing these changes, having to engage this new "digital native" mindset, people who think differently, process

differently and work differently. If you're sitting around having coffee with your middle level managers who are really working with these younger people, what advice would you pass on to them?

That's a really an interesting question. Times change and leaders need to change also. I would share and go back to some of the rules I've followed throughout my career. I actually picked some of these up from Jack Welch, the former General Electric CEO. The first rule is face reality as it is, not as you wish it were. Too often people face situations hoping for a particular outcome, but truly have no plan for dealing with all the different potential outcomes and the 2nd and 3rd order effects that may result. Hope is not a strategy. You need to face your situation head-on, face reality and then deal with it accordingly.

Another rule that Jack Welch had was to change before you have to. Many people are really reluctant to change, to do things differently. For whatever reason, they're stuck in old habits. It's difficult to change. You need to always be looking forward and adapting to what you think the future environment is going to be like. If you don't adjust and adapt, it might be too late once you get there. Leaders need to have a strategic vision. They need to have a long term plan and modify it as required. They need to look for ways that they can remain competitive i.e. cut costs, identify new markets, build the talent base and create new products. You have to continuously look at how you as an individual and how your organization can get better on a daily basis. Leadership needs to think globally, have an international perspective and think out of the box. Those are some of the most important things that I would say.

I like that phrase that "getting better daily". That's where our opportunities are. Every day it's getting up, looking for what you can do for your team and for yourself to move ahead.

Every day you should be going through that thought process. I think too often we get caught up in the operational tasks and we are not really reflective enough in doing solid thinking about, where we are, where we need to go, and what can we change to get better. There should be a conscious effort by each and every one of us to make that happen every day.

We are all our own worst critics. When you look back at both in your business and military experience, is there anything or any situation for which you would have prepared yourself differently or may have approached differently?

Like all of us, there are some things that I would do differently, but overall I don't really have any regrets about what I've accomplished. We all define success differently. To me, it's always been about being a good person, who does the right things and treats other people with respect and dignity and being someone who has the respect of his family, friends and coworkers. That being said, first of all, you need to manage your own career. Don't believe that if you do well, the system will take care of you.

The second thing is figure out what it is that you want to do and what your options are. Then develop a plan to get there. If you don't know where you're going, you'll never get there. Some people will say -- and I'm probably as guilty as anybody else -- "I'm not sure I know what it is that I want to do. I think I might want to be a lawyer, I think I might want to be a doctor, I think I might want to go in business" and so on. It's critical to just select a field and develop a plan for success. If you find out a little later that it's not the area that you want to work in, then adjust. Modify the plan and change it accordingly. But if you don't have a plan to start with, you'll never get there.

Third, build your network. Networking is incredibly important. You're not just asking somebody for a job. You're trying to get advice from that individual, somebody who is in a field that you want to get into, that you are potentially interested in. I would also say find a mentor. Develop a plan and set goals. Find out the requirements. For example, I read an interesting article by a retired Army brigadier general. He was the head of the Social Sciences Department at West Point and now he's the Director of the Yale Leadership Department. He was talking about military folks who transitioned to the civilian world and he commented, "One day you can't just wake up and decide I want to be a professor at a college or university. There are certain things you have to do to get there. You need a doctorate. You have to have extensive teaching experience. You have to have done scholarly research, i.e. publishing professional journals etc."

There are always exceptions to everything, but the bottom line is you need to prepare. Those things don't happen overnight. You need to set yourself up for success so you meet the requirements. You need to tell your superiors what you want to do. You can't assume that they know what it is that you want to do in terms of future assignments.

Humility is great and that's an important quality, but you need to let people know about your accomplishments and future desires. Don't be afraid to toot your horn once in a while. Diversify your skills and always strive to improve. There are people out there who let things happen to them. And then there are some people who make things happen. You want to be in the second category. Also, remember that the most important person in your career beside yourself is your immediate supervisor or your boss. You need to work on that relationship. You need to find a common bond. You need to see that person as an ally or partner and not as an adversary. The absolute worst jobs that I have had were those wherein that relationship was not where it needed to be for a variety of reasons. You need to communicate with your supervisor. Keep them informed and try to work with that individual. There may be some personality conflicts. You may not like their leadership style. But they are your boss. You have to adapt to them not vice versa. That's a very important point because your boss can make or break your career.

Steve, let me jump on that for a second. I think that's so important. What I'm finding in the business environment today is that some managers and supervisors are supervising younger people some of whom have no sense of deference. This is becoming quite a challenge for the managers and

leaders who sometimes are regarded as peers by the younger generation.

I think that goes back to the communication issue and clearly laying out what the expectations are when the individual is hired. I'm not so sure that always happens. It didn't always happen for me in the military. It didn't always happen for me in the business world. I think that the level of counselling and mentoring is key. It's not where it needs to be in most organizations, but it's getting better. For example, Lockheed Martin, where I currently work, recently instituted a system wherein you have to identify what your commitments are at the beginning of the year and again at the six month point. There is a midyear review and then an annual review. The process is much more detailed and thorough and structured than it used to be, but it's a good system because it gets managers and employees to interact. The bottom line is that one on one communication is so critical and needs to take place and it's the responsibility of the leader to drive that mindset.

Let me draw a picture and your response. You are sitting with a number of senior leaders and mid-level leaders. You are about to leave them and you want to ensure that they walk away with some key takeaway points. What would you say to them?

I would say you need to make leadership development a priority not just lip service. Leaders need to set the example. Leaders need to have a solid, well defined inclusive leadership development program that is clearly communicated to everyone. Leaders need to give everyone who so desires an opportunity to participate and compete in the program. Don't just focus on a few people, but on the organization as a whole. That needs to be part of the culture. Everyone needs to feel that they are or can be a leader. I know that everybody doesn't want to be a leader. They're happy being an individual contributor. But people want to have hope for a brighter future whatever that might be and they need to feel that they have a fair opportunity to compete. Without that hope, you will never get maximum performance. They'll just do what they have to do to get by. The greater the number of people with the leadership skills that your organization has, the higher the overall morale and performance.

One last thing. Having a reading program is very important. The Chief of Staff of the Army has a professional reading list. I've also seen that a few times in the corporate world, but not to the extent that they have in the military. There are several excellent books out there on leadership and management. Of note, there are two books that I wish I had read when I was 17 or 18 or younger as opposed to when I was in my late 50's. One is a classic by Dale Carnegie, "How to Win Friends and Influence People" originally written in 1936 and the second one is "The Ugly American" by William Lederer which was written in the 1950's. In both books, the central theme is that the key to success and effective leadership is relationships. "The Ugly American" covers relationships within the international context. That's important because we are engaging today more and more with people from different countries, cultures, ethnic backgrounds etc. The Dale Carnegie book focuses on day to day interactions and is just as relevant today as it was in 1936. It's all about the importance of relationships. One of the things that I've tried to guide my life by is that people want to feel special. They want to feel important. They want to feel like they are contributing. They want to be appreciated. They want to know that somebody cares about them. They don't care about your problems. They want you to hear about their problems. That's very fundamental. That's why you need to treat everybody with respect and dignity. You need to make everybody feel as if they are important and that they have something to contribute and that they count. Most importantly, they want someone to listen to them. Those points are critical to being an effective leader and to being successful in all aspects of your life. I'll end it there.

I think that's a great way to bring this whole conclusion. I have one very personal question. What's on the horizon for Steve Hashem? Do you plan to swim the English Channel? Do you plan to do some sailing?

To be honest with you, I'm kind of reaching a point in my career where I'm actually looking for a new challenge. I've been in the corporate world for 27 years and in the military for 37 years and I'd like to branch out into some other areas. It's important to me to help other people. I sit on the Board of Directors for a non-profit organization called Quantum Leap Farm. It's a community service organization that provides a variety of equine-assisted therapies to over 800 clients, many in law enforcement or wounded military veterans and their family members. QLF helps people of all ages and abilities grow strong, achieve goals and overcome challenges by engaging them with horses. It's a great organization and it's very satisfying for both Martha and me to be a part of it.

I'd like to get involved in additional non-profit endeavors that benefit the veteran community. Finally, I'm thinking about doing some teaching at a university or a college in the Philadelphia region in the management and leadership areas, maybe, even doing some coaching. I'm really passionate about leadership training and working and helping out young people. My parents were great, but neither one of them had a college education. I don't have any kids, but I've always liked working with young people to try to share with them some of the lessons and the experiences that I have learned. Parents are really important. As I mentioned earlier neither of my parents went to college. My dad had a scholarship to play football at Boston College, but he couldn't go because he had eight brothers and sisters. He was the oldest one and he had to work to support the family. Just because someone doesn't go to college, doesn't mean that they're not intelligent or wise. I learned a lot from my parents, but there were three lessons that I learned that were more important than any knowledge that I gained from a textbook or academic instruction. First is integrity. Second is meeting your commitments. And third is the importance of diversity and racial equality.

Lesson #1… be honest. When I was a little kid …. probably seven or eight years old, there was a grocery store up the street on the corner. One day, I stole a box of matches from the store and I walked home. My mother saw me. She asked "what are you doing, where did you get those". So I told her what I had done. I could tell that she was very angry. She grabbed me by the collar and dragged me back up to the store, made me return them and apologize to the owner. The second lesson was from my dad. He had just returned home after World War II where he had served as an enlisted soldier. Shortly after his return, he applied for a job at the local post office. In the interim, he also applied for a job at a tannery and he accepted the job there because after several days he hadn't heard anything from the post office. A few days later someone from the post office called and offered him a job there. He told the post office, "I'm sorry, but I've already accepted a job, I'm already committed to work at the leather tannery". Well he took that job at the tannery and stayed there for 37 years, working every day with nasty dyes and chemicals. I worked there myself for a couple of summers and it was not a very healthy work environment. But he made a commitment to the tannery. So that's why he stayed there, even though long term the post office would have been a much more beneficial and healthier job. That's not to say that he couldn't have left after a few years, but he decided to stay because he had made a commitment.

Lesson #2 is meet your commitments. The third lesson involved some of my relatives, who quite frankly were prejudiced against minorities. They would frequently make some very negative remarks toward minorities, Hispanics, African Americans, etc. I would tag along with my parents and brother to visit these relatives, primarily uncles and aunts, every weekend for probably 15 years until I went away for college. Some of these relatives would make these disparaging comments and both my father and mother would stand up to them and say "That's wrong. Every one of us is equal regardless of background should be treated the same. You are no better than they are." They very easily could have said nothing or could have just said, "You're right". However, they stood up for what was really right which was treating everybody with respect and dignity and as an equal.

So lesson #3 was be tolerant and accepting of diversity and treat all people with respect and dignity regardless of background, race or color. I could probably tell you a lot of other things that I learned, but those were probably the three most important ones that have made a significant and lasting impact on my life. No doubt parents can make a big difference in their children's lives in both a positive or negative manner. Thank God I was very fortunate to have wonderful parents who I owe a lot to.

Steve, thank you very much for your service to our country and for your contribution to this effort.

Thank you, Kevin, for including me in this initiative. What you are doing is very important and will be very beneficial to many people.

Chapter 8: Let Them Stumble, Practice, and Fail…Good Leaders Will Press On

Pete Marshall
Former Vice Commander
Naval Facilities Engineering Command

Meet Pete Marshall, Rear Admiral (ret) now serving as a senior consultant in the design and construction industry. Pete has more than 40 years experience in design, construction and facilities management, successfully demonstrating the full range of facilities acquisition, engineering and quality assurance expertise. His Navy background of 32 years started with assignment to the Navy's military construction forces, the Seabees, and U.S. Naval Mobile Construction Battalion FIFTY-EIGHT, where he participated in a deployment to Chu Lai, Republic of Vietnam, throughout 1969. Further Seabee assignments included: Officer in Charge of Underwater Construction

Team TWO, Commanding Officer of Amphibious Construction Battalion ONE, Commander of the Twenty-second Naval Construction Regiment, and Commander of the Third Naval Construction Brigade. He had two additional command assignments: Commanding Officer of the Public Works Center, San Francisco Bay and Commander of Pacific Division, Naval Facilities Engineering Command. Completing postgraduate education with a master's degree in ocean engineering at the University of Rhode Island in 1974, Pete subsequently interspersed tours as diving officer and ocean engineer in the Naval Facilities Engineering Command's Ocean Facilities Program. These included project officer at Chesapeake Division, Naval Facilities Engineering Command; Undersea Surveillance Officer at Naval Electronics Systems Command Headquarters, Washington, D.C.; and Director of the Ocean Facilities Program at Naval Facilities Engineering Command headquarters, 1987-1990. After retiring from the Navy in 2000, Pete worked as a corporate officer for Parsons Brinckerhoff, Burns and Roe, and Dewberry. He is a registered Professional Engineer in the states of California and Virginia and is qualified as a Seabee Combat Warfare Officer. He also serves as the chair of the Federal Facilities Council of the National Research Council which is a board of facility executives across various federal agencies predominately in the National Capital Region around Washington, DC.

AUTHOR NOTE: I have had the recent privilege of working alongside Pete in his role as chairman of the Federal Facilities Council of the National Research Council. He has brought a number of skills to the table in managing this body to include establishing a consensus agenda for research priories that the Council needs to address.

Pete, thanks again for taking your time to share your thoughts on leadership development. As a senior level leader what do you see as the core responsibilities of senior leaders in bringing growth to organizations and raising up leaders?

I think I'll rephrase the question a little bit. I believe what you need to be doing is to respect and develop all your people. Not everybody in your organization will become a leader. In addition, not everybody in your organization wants to become a leader. But they all need to have the right seat on the bus and feel as if they are making a real contribution to the organization. I find it unfortunate that much of our historic reward, promotion, or recognition mechanisms are really focused on leadership. You are promoted because the organization wants you to move up and be a leader. Even compensation mechanisms sometimes work in similar ways. But what we truly need to do is to dictate a broader involvement.

For example, I come out of the engineering profession. I have had junior people working for me who had absolutely no desire to become a senior leader. All they wanted to do was become the best structural engineer in the world. You have got to figure out a way to satisfy that person's needs. He or she may not become a leader. Nonetheless we need to let them fulfill his or her desires. The added benefit in doing this is that, when you sit down and work through the development of all your people, you start to whittle down the group of those folks who really desire to be a leader. Once this is accomplished, you now have identified a core pool of people in whom you can invest that specific leadership process. I'm not recommending that this has to be some grand formal system. You don't need books of personnel development or folders on everybody. But, you do need to have an understanding of your folks; on how they desire to fit in and grow. And you need to make sure they all have some professional development mechanisms available that enhance their respective growth. If you do that, you have taken a significant step up in investing in all your people.

In respect to the development of your leaders, this development comes from at least three elements that I can identify. The first is knowledge derived from education, training, on the job experience and routinely some common sense. The second element is opportunity. And the last one is luck.

The education is essential, actually compulsory, as it is vital for opening the door for someone to enter that pool of potential leaders. If your profession or your career at the top level requires a bachelor's degree or a master's degree, it is vital that the individual pursue and secure that credential. Training and on the job experience are something that senior leaders can assist with. And then, routine common sense is critical. A potential leader needs to be able to separate the wheat from the chaff early on, demonstrating basic knowledge and the capacity to turn in the correct direction when faced with a decision.

Some of the opportunities that a leader is faced with are external. They are thrust upon him or her and offer an opportunity to excel. For example, today you have an excellent example of an external opportunity. We have base commanders in Gulfport MS which, after this weekend, will have a reputation for handling themselves in a hurricane. It may be a good reputation or a bad reputation but they are going to have a reputation, a resume for disaster preparedness, disaster recovery, emergency management, and so on. That's an opportunity that is forced upon them. They may have some previous training and experience but this weather challenge will bring out their capacity to respond in the situation. It will be telltale.

Pete, just to provide a timeline perspective, as of this writing, it is August 28th, 2012, the eve of Hurricane Isaac which has yet to make landfall.

Kevin, thank you for providing that reference point. Now let's move to internal opportunities. Internal opportunities are something that a senior leader can make available to the junior leaders. External opportunities are circumstantial or environmental whereas internal opportunities can be stimulated by the senior leader.

And the last element is luck. I don't want to stress that too much. But in reality, we have all sat around, witnessed situations that haven't been good and say 'but for the grace of God that could have been me not long ago'. There are times in my history that I have made a decision on a Monday that worked and worked well. But on a Tuesday or a Wednesday or Thursday, it never would have worked, because the circumstances just were not lined up the same way. The circumstances were just slightly different and I just happened to be at the right place at the right time.

Now what does a senior leader do? A senior leader must be able to evaluate juniors as potential leaders, to make a determination about their potential, and proactively influence their training and internal opportunities for growth. To that extent, you are now able to assist those potential leaders to come along in their professional development. You can mentor them. If that is not possible, you need to have an honest conversation about where that person best fits within the organization and where they want to go in their life and career. Maybe they are not meant to be a successful senior leader. Sometimes those conversations can be as important to the organization and to the individual as almost anything else.

I believe that most folks want to be the best at what they do. It just so happens that not everyone wants to become an organization's senior leader, whereas others may be aspiring to move up the leadership scale. The key here is to be able to discern the individual's real desires and capabilities.

Another characteristic I would look for is adaptability. That is being able to handle different circumstances that are either thrust upon them by me as a leader or situations that they experience as a part of their work environment and how they handle those changes and challenges. I also look for people that learn from their mistakes from a broad perspective. Let me offer an example. I was managing a utility company overseas and we had an above–ground, closed-in reservoir. One of the people that managed it told me that they had measured the contents of the tank using a sounding technique and determined that the tank was almost empty. However, the tank had an outside gauge indicating that it was full. Nonetheless, they used this sound technique means of inspection which marked them as empty. Thus, because of the empty tank indication and under my direction, we put out water restriction qualifications. Later, my boss asked the most telling and simple question: Had I looked in the tank to see firsthand what was happening to correlate the variances between the two readings. The answer was no. I trusted my folks. I decided to conduct a personal inspection and found out that the tanks were, in fact, full. The outside gauge was correct. Upon further inspection, I determined that we were using a flawed method of sounding the tank's content. Beyond learning about the problem with our tank sounding techniques, what I did learn was, to the best of my ability, I was not going to take a problem up my chain of command (i.e. putting out water restrictions) without personally validating the problem.

As you get more senior, your ability to understand firsthand and to intimately get engaged with every problem diminishes because your sphere of influence and range of responsibility grow. But at the same time, you can instill confidence in your people and exhort them to understand what the true problem is. Don't just be a courier of the last message you have received. You've got to get more intimately involved.

So that's what I mean by the ability to learn from mistakes. I want them to learn beyond the specifics of the mistake and the error. I want them to grow and understand the bigger issue. In my case, it was not to simply understand the reservoir logistics per se but to understand how important it is to be able to demonstrate a comprehension of the problem and provide some value to the solutions, not simply be a conduit of information flow.

The other important item is the potential to grow. The Core Competencies Study conducted by the National Research Council displayed a competency chart, showing essentially four skill sets for a technical senior manager and how they changed over time, spanning the period from completing a college degree through becoming a CEO. The four skill sets were technical skills, supervisory skills, managerial skills and enterprise skills. The degree to which each of these skill sets applies varies through your career. For junior folks, technical skills are high priority because you are just commencing your career and you have probably been employed because of those particular technical skills. Neither supervising nor managing is in the mix at this stage. Over the course of time as you work your way up in an organization as a leader, the technical skills become less important. But the managerial and enterprise skills become more essential. This progression and recognition of the application of these skill sets provide a great backdrop for a conversation with junior personnel to determine whether they desire to remain on a technical track or are more interested in moving towards management. It focuses them on where they truly want to go and what they want to do.

And that leads into the kind of training that should be provided to them. What kind of challenges will they rise to? I mentioned earlier that much of this applies to you as a senior leader as you are developing your emerging leaders. Nonetheless, each person does have some compulsory actions to address. As I came up in the Navy, it was compulsory for me to obtain a professional engineering license. It was a requirement for promotion on the technical side as well as to become a senior leader. The Navy helped me. They would provide some courses. They would pay for courses. They would give me a little bit of study time. But at the end of the day it was up to me to achieve the professional registration. The PE registration was a compulsory for me to achieve. Then there are the non-compulsory activities which were those professional/internal growth opportunities that my senior leaders provided to me. As I progressed in my career, I then endeavored to provide the same opportunities for my up and coming juniors.

You've made it clear that the individual has responsibilities for continued success. And the organization certainly has a shared responsibility. Is there anything that you would highlight from your military experience or your business experience that organizations could do better in ensuring that success is occurring for those growing leaders?

Yes...absolutely. Looking back at my last ten years in the Navy and ten years subsequent in private practice, we seemed to have developed an aversion to taking risk, a fear of failure. I completely understand that you can't have major failure. You don't want a system to exist where, for example, someone could die or state secrets are being compromised or disclosed, particularly if you're in the government. But I can recall so many times throughout my junior career where I was given tasks and I was allowed to work through the task. If it wasn't the desired result, I would be mentored at how to get a better result or how a process improvement could have gotten me a better result. My earlier discussion on the reservoir problem is an example. Today, I see less of that. Fear of failure eats away at an organization and it eats away at the capacity to really develop successful future senior leaders. This fear of failure also encourages micromanagement by seniors which can erode any initiative that junior leaders may take. This erodes any capacity or opportunity for junior leaders to make mistakes and learn from them.

Just think of the result: As the senior leadership with micromanaging tendencies retires, juniors haven't developed the capacity to recognize the value found in making mistakes and learning from them. They get promoted fearful of making those mistakes, fearing that a senior failure is typically much worse than a junior failure. Suddenly, now you have this organization that hasn't experienced any of the learning curve. In addition, they are paralyzed from this fear of failure. And what you really find is that you have an organization filled with followers and very few leaders. Trust and confidence are sorely lacking. You don't know who you can count on, who's been tested under fire and knows how to move on and handle problems, and who is adaptable.

You've got to allow the juniors and the organization to push that bubble so they can make mistakes, to test their thinking at the lower level, to learn from it, and then to move on. Again I'm not talking about letting somebody fail when the potential result is going to cause death and destruction or total failure of the organization. What I am saying is that you must let your junior leaders' capabilities be tested. They will learn, grow, move on, and move up in the organization and move up in their learning curves.

You touched on something I'd like to get your thoughts on and that has to do with just how rapidly our business world is changing today. The technological aspects of it. You made the point that people, sometimes by accident, fall into micromanaging people because of their ability to touch them too quickly and so often. And it can erode the ability of someone to grow. I'm seeing that myself in my own business environment. What would you say to those growing leaders today, who are coming up the ranks, about how they can best manage those relationships given how technology has exploded?

Just because you can interfere doesn't mean you should. You have to hold back, and allow people to develop somewhat on their own. I had a boss call me one day wanting an answer to a problem. I said 'fine...I'll get you the answer'. He then started to beat me up politely, telling me that I should know the answer since I was a senior engineer. I told him that I did know the answer but the issue wasn't for me to provide the answer in 25 seconds or less. But rather the issue is for me to go to my people and say the big boss is interested in this issue. Here are the parameters. Go find out what's happening. Give me the answer so I can pass it on. That response got a lot of silence from the big boss. Nonetheless he concurred that I was right.

Even though you can pick up the phone and get an immediate answer, no matter where you stand in that chain of command or in the hierarchy, there are times when you must let the system work in order to develop your people. Those are hard decisions if you're the manager of the juniors. Those are hard decisions if you are the CEO and you want the answer right away. But there comes a time when you really have to understand that we are talking about development and training, a lot of bringing people along. That doesn't happen over a 25 second phone call with someone blurting out the answer. It's always enticing, if you know the answer to give that answer to your boss and move on with life. But, when you do so, the juniors are left out and never even know that the CEO asked for the answer. They just keep going about their job. It takes time to let the juniors develop. You must get them engaged so they can start that process, learn it, and come to you with what they believe the answer is. If they come back with an incomplete or wrong answer, you now can discuss how they got there. You can now offer help because they will be more inclined to receive such help. You can also demonstrate a little patience and understanding.

I think you get a sense that I have spent a career rebelling against micro management. I tried my best to never go back and do the job I had previously completed. As I moved from being a company commander to a battalion commander, I never wanted to go back and be a company commander. I enjoyed doing it but after promotion I tried to let my company commanders be company commanders, to learn through their own mistakes. When I went up to the regiment I never wanted to go back and be a battalion commander because I had already done that. I had the t-shirt. I wanted to move on and I wanted to let those other people learn. Fortunately for most of my career, I didn't have cell phones available. So the rapid communication up and down wasn't as immediate as it is now. You just have to put that temptation aside and let people work themselves through life as long as it's not a fatal flaw. I had a boss who even told me once that as long as I was not going to hurt anybody or give away classified information, everything else could be corrected after the fact. He worked with me that way. I thought that was an interesting comment on life. I've tried to emulate some of that.

One of the biggest challenges in leadership today is that brand new leader who is supervising a group of people for the first time. What would you tell them to be thinking about as they start to build a relationship with that new organization that he or she is managing?

Well I think there are several elements. One is to remember what got you to where you are. Who you respected and who you learned from positively and negatively. Think back to those whom you did not like and why. Sometimes there are things you don't like but once you move up in the organization or you hit that next step, you come to understand why they were doing what they were doing. In turn, if there wasn't a good understanding or if his or her style happened to work for a bad or poor supervisor, then okay. You can still be a different person.

The second is more a matter of staying relevant and connected with the folks you're supervising. I'm not saying you have to be one of the guys because you don't. In fact you shouldn't. But you have to understand the working relationships and your people's common interests. So you have to stay relevant in their eyes across the board on all parts and pieces. Culturally, socially, you've got to know what's going on. As soon as you become detached, then you've lost the bubble and it becomes very difficult to be a good supervisor or leader when you don't have that identity for what they are going through, what they have gone through, and what they aspire to do.

One other element is that you must understand that you are always mentoring because you are the example. They will walk your talk, to use old terminology. It's how you dress. It's how you behave. It's how you speak and act. It's how you arrive at work. As a mid-level or senior manager, if you don't like what you see in your people, my advice would be to take a look in the mirror. People are emulating you because you are the senior. You are always the example. You don't have to become paranoid over that. You just have to be comfortable in your skin and understand that you're out there and they are looking at you and you are their leader. Regardless of what level you are within the organization.

People are looking at you whether you are having a direct conversation with them or not. They are watching you through your work day and through your habits and how to respond to issues.

And it's good and bad. It's not insidious. It's just always there. For example, I think I always worked hard in my jobs. And I put in a lot of hours but I was as rigorous as I could ever be at leaving the office at a rational hour in the afternoon or early evening. I would say 5 or 6. The reason being, if I stayed in the office late, people had this impression that they had to be in the office late.

As I got to be more senior particularly in the military, there was staff there that would also be in the office late with me. Well what message are you sending about your life as a senior leader if some junior is looking and feeling that he has to work 18 hours a day? He starts to think 'I'm not so sure I want to do that to my family and for the rest of my life'. If had more work to do, I might go home and do it. But I'd do it on my own and quietly. The only person I would have to deal with was my wife. But for the most part, I wanted to make sure that the people around me were living a rational life and seeing that I was having fun and that there were other things going on in my life; that I was not just a taskmaster to what was office work on a routine basis. That doesn't mean that there were times that I had to be there in emergencies and major operations. Sure…that happens at times. You've got to do what makes it work. But there's a temptation to become a slave to administrative work that is never ending. You can never get all the admin work done. I don't care who you are or how long you spend. So you have to declare victory and separate yourself from it after a reasonable amount of time. As long as there wasn't something critical that needed my yes or no, then I could go home, live my life, and I could come back the next day to pick up and continue on. And in turn, everybody who was working for me could go home and have a life

Those are words of wisdom that you just said there. Let me ask this as we coming to the end here. We are all our own worst critics. We can beat ourselves up forever over decisions we have made or things we did and so on. As we go on the road of life, we can look back and regain perspective and see things we might have changed. Looking back at the challenges you have faced in your career, is there anything that jumps out at you where you might say 'I might have prepared or approached this differently now that I know what I know'? Does anything come to mind along those lines?

There's not much I would change. I would say if there's anything that jumps out at me looking back on the 40 years, it's the importance of open communications. As an aspiring junior leader, you've got to be able to talk honestly about what you want to do and where you are going. And then as a senior leader, you've got to be able to effectively and openly communicate all of those issues with your folks. I tried to be open. I think I did a good job. But communication is one of those things I'm not sure you can ever do enough. I probably can give you examples where I communicated with my people too much. They started to understand almost immediately what I was going to say every time I opened my mouth on an issue because I was consistent for months, saying the same thing. But in dealing with personal development, it's sometimes a difficult conversation with people. Particularly with individuals who you get a sense don't have the tools to succeed in the direction they have chosen and really need to be looking at something else. Those are times when you need to sit down and pull up the open communication book and have a long conversation.

I had an aspiring company commander who was just not doing well. He was not in the company command position yet, but we were going to put him there. And it looked like this was going to be certain failure and embarrassment to a lot of folks. So I brought him in and we talked, it must have been 4 hours. As we got to the end of the conversation he said 'you know I just want to be an engineer. I don't want to be in charge. I don't want to supervise. I'm not really comfortable being in the military'. It was a bit of a revelation to both of us and because of that conversation, he ended up leaving the Navy. He was coming up on a decision point in his naval career and his decision was to leave. I found that 4 hour conversation to be really interesting and revealing even though it was somewhat painful to go through. About two years later I bumped into him at an airport. I wasn't sure what he was going to say but he was delighted. He was working in an engineering firm as an engineer on a CAD machine. He wasn't supervising anybody. He wasn't filling out any personnel evaluations. He wasn't trying to lead a crew. And he couldn't have been happier with life. That made me feel good. Sometimes those tough communication situations can be the most rewarding. Long way around the barn here to say that you need to take time and communicate. It's important to talk to people particularly on the issue of personnel development.

I would say that the conversation you had with him is the kind of conversation that is probably critical in those beginning stages. As you said earlier in our discussion, it is important to identify who really wants to move on and be a leader and who doesn't. And that saves your organization and people a lot of time and pain.

Absolutely. You want to identify the people who do want to move up and who you think have those skill sets. And sometimes you want their skill sets beyond the position they currently occupy because you can recognize them as natural supervisors and managers. Some of them have enterprise skill sets already as a junior. If you can identify those early, take advantage of that. No matter what organization you are in, military, civilian, anywhere. You want those people to rise up and move along. I think I said it at the beginning. You'll get other people who have no interest, who do not want to be a supervisor. Okay. We still might have a seat on the bus for them. And we'll develop them in a different manner.

Let me ask you a wrap up question here. What do you see on the horizon in business now in this area of leadership development? Just what challenges do you see in that area? What flags would you wave in front of people to be paying attention to?

Well I'll have to go back and repeat maybe in different words one of the earlier items. As you craft a development plan for your juniors, recognize that some do want to be leaders and some don't. Then you've got to let them learn, you've got to have a system that lets them stumble. They need to practice and fail. You must instill confidence and develop the trust needed so they will succeed as they come up that chain. Don't expect perfection. And you can't be there to punish them at every learning error. As long as the error isn't extremely critical, you can provide latitude for them to learn from their errors. This fear of failure and risk aversion is negatively impacting too many organizations. You've got to let people develop on their own, to stumble and dust off, get up, and press on. Everybody learns from that and that is really essential for development of personnel and for development of strong organizations.

Pete, I want to thank you for your service to our country and for participating in this project. I believe many people are going to benefit from this as you have laid out very practical advice and guidance, something I know people are wanting to hear.

Kevin, it has been my pleasure

Chapter 9: Proceed Until Apprehended

Dave Nash

Former Commander

Naval Facilities Engineering Command

Meet Dave Nash, Rear Admiral (ret) now serving as the CEO for an enterprise within the biofuels industry. Dave has over four decades of experience in building, design and program management for both the U.S. Navy and the private sector. His experience includes the management of multi-billion dollar physical asset programs, including the U.S. Navy's shore installations worldwide and the reconstruction of Iraq's infrastructure. Dave served as Director of the Iraq Program Management Office (PMO) under the Coalition Provisional Authority and later, as Director of the Iraq Reconstruction Management Office (IRMO) under the U.S. State Department. Under his direction, these organizations managed the $18.4 billion Iraq infrastructure reconstruction.

Dave is currently the President of Sustainable Biofuels Solutions (SBS), LLC. SBS does research and development; sales and marketing; project development; manufacturing; installation and operation of waste to energy plants throughout the world. Prior to assuming the leadership of SBS, Dave served as the Chairman and CEO of Dave Nash and Associates International, LLC, a premier project development firm he founded, providing turn-key services to businesses and governments that seek support on bioenergy, energy and large infrastructure projects in emerging markets. He also served as the Chairman and CEO Jordan - BE&K Federal Services, LLC, a company focused on the Federal Construction market.

AUTHOR NOTE: I had the privilege of working alongside Dave as a senior program officer when he led the National Research Council study entitled "Core Competencies for Federal Facilities Asset Management Through 2020: Transformational Strategies". He very effectively modeled a collaborative style of leadership that is critical in such a consensus – building environment. He did so while still keeping a firm grip on the tiller, steering the study committee in the right direction. This was particularly noteworthy given some headwinds that he faced in building the necessary consensus, which ultimately resulted in recommendations that have been utilized across government and within the facility asset management domain.

Dave, thanks for being a part of this leadership development research effort. Let me move right into our discussion. Organizations today must be able to raise up new leaders. As a senior level

leader, you've been charged with the responsibility of accomplishing this for the various organizations for which you have worked. What do you see as those core responsibilities that senior leaders have to make this mission of raising up new leaders happen?

The thing that comes to mind immediately is that it is not about me as a senior leader. It is about the organization or the entity that you're leading. It will not survive unless you bring along those leaders who will take your place in the future. One of the things that dawned on me early in my military career is that a military person trains their relief or trains their replacement. So the focus has to be placed on identifying and developing your replacement. By doing this, you ensure that the organization gets the right kind of leadership. It's more about the people that they lead than the leader themselves.

In terms of looking for people who you feel can step up into a leadership role, what do you look for in that individual?

First of all I think I have a view that maybe not all the academics agree with. I'm a believer that you can make great leaders out of good leaders, but you can't make good leaders out of bad leaders. What I look for is their ability to relate to others. It is how you get along. In the military and in the private sector, I've seen those people who strive to get ahead of everybody else. They tend not to do very well. It's my opinion that it's your peers who propel you along the road to success. Just competing at any cost doesn't work.

The second thing I look for is somebody that thrives on responsibility. They have no fear. That has its downsides. They will bump their head against things on occasion. If you're going to help them, you have to know when they are in extremis and when they are not. You have to understand that you mature as a leader. You don't start out as a great leader. You've got to mature as a leader. It's experiential as much as, and possibly even more than, it is educational. It's very important to give them the opportunity to try things on. The last thing I look for in people are those who are engaged in the mission of the entity and not just themselves. They understand that we succeed through teamwork. We succeed through everybody succeeding. People that can encourage that or can develop that kind of strong feeling in their peers is the kind of person who will succeed as a leader in my experience.

Organizations can miss the mark at times in raising up leaders. Where do you see organizations missing the mark when it comes to raising up that next generation of leaders?

I think it has partly to do with the size of the organization. Huge organizations have a harder time with developing leaders for several reasons. First, it is hard to know everybody. It's hard to come up with a process that really works. I was associated with a process one time where they would select people that they thought had potential. Unfortunately, the people who recommended these individuals weren't very judicious in picking out those who they thought might succeed. They would do it as sort of a gift to their friends, or a gift to their colleague that they wanted to see move ahead. Someone who wasn't necessarily prepared to become a leader. Organizations that are large have a very difficult time.

In addition, risk is managed in a different way in large organizations. If you want to develop leaders, you've got to be willing to take some risk. Not dumb risk but smart risk where you allow people to engage in situations that might be a little over their head and may have a little bit of downside risk. If you can help them get through that, then they become better leaders. They experience something, and they learn. Certainly you don't want them to learn with catastrophic failure.

You've also got to have an organization that has a sense about what really counts and what doesn't count, in terms of success and failure. Large organizations once again have a very difficult time with that because they are looking for process and for a way to make sure things don't happen. They can't afford all those risks. I think a smaller organization, in terms of managing risk, is probably in a better position to develop leaders. Of course they have less resources and therefore can't provide as big a challenge or opportunity. I think organizations that are huge have an inertia problem. They tend to be on a march to somewhere. As such, it's very hard for them to accommodate people that have new ideas about how to manage or how to do things. Innovation in large organizations is much harder than it is in small agile type organizations.

Finally, I would say that the real difference between organizations that develop leaders and those that don't is a mindset. You, the senior leader, have to create the environment in which those who will be the leaders of the future can thrive. If you don't do that, and all you do is worry about quarterly results or worry about yourself, that usually puts an organization in failure mode.

One last thing that I would say is that organizations that are privately held often have a hard time with transition of ownership which is really the transition of leadership, if you will. Those who created or founded the organization tend to keep too tight a grip on it. When it comes time for them to retire, or they get removed from the situation by some other event, the organization flounders. It flounders, because there is nobody to pick up the mantle and move on. It is essential to create an environment where leaders can learn and thrive over time.

You talked about dumb versus smart risk, risk aversion, and how certain things can creep into an organization that can hinder development. How can organizations ensure that the culture can be the enabler, if you will, so new leaders can emerge effectively?

I think one way is communications. I know that's an overused word. If you have an environment where people will openly communicate about how things are going and how they feel about things, you can obtain helpful and critical feedback. An individual has their own perspective of how things are going. It's very seldom the way everybody else feels. The second thing is that you have to be flexible as a senior leader. You have to come to the conclusion that you don't know everything.

When I first entered the Navy, I thought that, in order to succeed, I'd have to have all the bright ideas in the world. I ran out of bright ideas in about 30 seconds. I decided that the way to do it was to work with others and to collaborate. So I think you need to engender an environment of collaboration within the organization. People will then feel free to come together and will not be threatened by somebody else who might want get ahead of them because they will be going against the grain of the collaborative culture. Open communication, a collaborative environment, and a willingness to take chances and embrace responsibility. To me those are the keys to creating an environment where bold, bright new leaders will emerge.

Another issue you touched on indirectly is the sharing of knowledge. I'd be interested in your views on how a senior leader can contribute to that process of knowledge sharing so that leaders are being properly equipped.

If a senior leader is truly a leader and is willing to share and is not threatened by his or her subordinates or peers, they will embrace the process of knowledge sharing and will seek opportunities to communicate. I've been in some organizations where the CEO used to meet with a cadre of young team members or employees. That was good, and that was not so good. That was good, because it gave the young people an opportunity to see what the end game looks like, in terms of the kinds of things that they would be asked to deal with when they become seniors. It has a down side in that whoever you pick to be a part of that group then becomes the "defacto anointed". By doing that, you may miss some people who have great talent but become disheartened and go somewhere else. The senior leadership in an organization must develop an awareness of what they are willing to share and when and with whom that sharing is appropriate.

As I've advanced, and I guess I'm in my old age now, I'm a believer that you always tell the truth. You don't have to hide things. Obviously, there are some things that you shouldn't share. That's obvious. The more you tell people about what's going on, the more they are engaged. In smaller organizations it's very easy to do. In a larger organization, it's very hard to do. You have to use different mechanisms, different processes, but you've got to be willing to share. If you're not willing to share, then everybody feels like they're out of the loop, and they begin to complain. They think that other people know things that they don't know. It's really important.

Our youngest son is involved in applying the social network approach to a business, and that's a threat to old people like me, because everybody knows everything. It gives them an opportunity to share their ideas. It also, if handled correctly, creates an environment where excellent, outstanding new ideas emerge that the senior leader never would have thought of in a hundred years. It's not to denigrate the knowledge of the senior leader. Sometimes as a senior leader, you don't see things when you're there near the top that people see that are not near the top. I think that's a possibility for the future, that is, the ability to communicate freely across the organization.

One organization I was in had various networks they put together on various technical issues. If somebody out in the field of this 20,000-person company had a difficult question or a difficult project problem, they could send it to this network. I was amazed at how everybody just loved that. They would participate and they would not give up until they had solved the problem. I think there are many ways to communicate. You've got to be willing to share as an organization or an organizational leader. If not, all you will get is this sort of employee-boss kind of relationship where people simply come to work for eight hours a day. As a result, all they are really interested in is their paycheck.

It's interesting that you mention the social networking environment. The environments in the business world have shifted drastically in the last ten years. This shift is reflected in how the younger generation sees their roles and relationships with leadership. And we also have new technological tools and the challenges that they bring. Given your recent experiences, how can leaders prepare themselves to adjust to those kinds of challenges?

You were with me when we were doing the Core Competencies study. One of the things that was interesting to me is that there's a block of obsolescence. There's a large group of people in the federal government who are reaching retirement. They're all going to go out the door, and the federal government has not been able to hire the replacements and work them up through the system. There's this great fear about all this corporate knowledge walking out the door. This study concluded that this was bad news and it was good news. It was bad news from the standpoint that much would be lost and a lot of great employees would be gone. What

135

they knew and what they could do would no longer be available to the federal government.

On the other hand, we would be bringing in young people who are very comfortable in the digital age who have grown up learning that that is the way you communicate, express your ideas, and find solutions. The older gang, like me, is technologically challenged. The new group comes in and is quite comfortable with all the mechanisms and gadgets we have around to help us today. It's sort of a mixed blessing. I think the key to this is that the senior level needs to understand that they process things differently from younger people. The core basics are still there about leadership, how you communicate, how to deal with people, and all those sorts of things.

But I think there's a merging of capabilities between the older entities of people, who are more traditional in their communication. Couple that with the ability to move information and ideas at light speed across vast networks. If you can meld those two together, then the transition is an improvement, with the next generation taking over an environment that has become enhanced. As long as some of the basics such as human relations and collaborative communications are transferred, then the young people will bring their new skills and make the overall environment a richer one. An organization has to create an environment wherein there is a willingness to listen to new ideas and new ways of communicating and new ways of decision making. At the same time, it is vital to keep your hands on the real basics of being ethical and humane.

If you could turn back the clock and maybe change how you prepared yourself for the challenges that have come your way, what changes do you think you might have made?

I wouldn't have made any changes because I think part of learning is experiential. It's not something you get out of books or you get from somebody telling you. I've made my share of mistakes and tried to learn from every one. I don't think you can become a good leader out of a book. I think you have to experience various and sundry things as you go through your career. If you learn from it and adapt and improve your style, you will continue to thrive. If you don't, you'll be stuck forever where you are. We can both think of examples of both extremes of that, so I wouldn't change anything. I've never been prepared for anything I've done, but I've been willing to keep at it. My motto is "proceed until apprehended," and I have not been apprehended yet. I don't mean that in an illegal sort of way. I mean that you've got to be willing to go ahead and give it your best. Sometimes you fall short and sometimes you don't. You figure out what really transpired, what you could have done differently, and what you should do differently the next time. That's the way I go through life. It does not mean that I've had a perfect career as a leader. As I said, I've made my share of mistakes, but I've tried to learn from each one.

As we wind up, let me paint a picture for you and let you respond to it. You're in a room with all manner and levels of leaders, senior leaders, midlevel, and emerging leaders. You're trying to leave them with a final thought. I'm sure you've

137

heard people say, "If you forget everything I have said, remember this." What would you say to people today, if you were to leave them or charge them with some final thoughts on leadership?

I would advise them to accept their responsibilities as a leader to prepare those who will come after them, and I would leave it at that.

Okay, well that's great. I've got one other personal question since I've been on the sidelines watching you move ahead. You've got this new company you're starting up. Are there any other things you intend to do like swim the English Channel or sail a boat around the horn of Africa or anything like that you're trying to get done?

I have a very simple motto and that is "I want to die on a dead run doing something appropriate." That may not be a very high bar to jump over, but I've retired twice as I said. I'm going to keep going until I don't find it fun anymore, and I don't want to get up and go to work. I enjoy interactions with people. I enjoy challenges, and as long as I'm able to do it, and do it as best I can, I'm going to keep at it.

Dave, let me conclude by saying again thank you. Thank you for your service to the country. Thank you for being a part of this effort.

Thank you very much. I appreciate being a part.

Chapter 10: Meet Change Head On...and Embrace It

Gregory Schumacher
Former Commanding General
Military Intelligence Readiness Command, U.S. Army

Meet Greg Schumacher, Major General (ret) now serving as an executive in the cyber-intel world. Greg joined Scitor Corporation on 1 February 2012 where he serves as Director for Army Programs and Defense Intelligence initiatives. His activities include business development, cyber initiatives, and strategic outreach and integration. Prior to joining Scitor, he served the U.S. Army for 37 years in key command and staff assignments, primarily in Military Intelligence. He had two brigade commands, including the 201st Military Intelligence Brigade at Ft. Lewis, WA, and served as the Deputy Chief of Staff for Intelligence for the Army Reserve Command at Ft. McPherson, GA. Upon selection for promotion to Brigadier General, he stood up and commanded the Military Intelligence Readiness Command, the first of its kind national, functional intelligence organization in the Army Reserve. The formation of this command provided an unprecedented level of partnership between the Active Army and the Army Reserve intelligence formations, resulting in a level of support to Operations Iraqi Freedom and Enduring Freedom that were previously unattainable. He culminated his Army career as the Assistant Deputy Chief of Staff for Intelligence, Headquarters, Department of the Army, at the Pentagon. Greg has a Bachelor of Science degree from the United States Military Academy at West Point and a Master's Degree in Education from Texas Tech University. He currently serves on the Board for Freedom Ranch, a non-profit corporation dedicated to providing respite and restoration for those Wounded Warriors who reach the limits of their abilities to cope after transitioning back to civilian life.

Greg, thank you for participating in this leadership research project. Let's dive in. Organizations are constantly faced with raising up new leaders. This is vital for growth, vital for them to meet their mission, to meet their goals. Clearly senior leaders have a role in that. I'd like to get your thoughts on what you see as the core responsibilities for senior leaders to help grow that next generation of leaders and making that happen.

It is vital for senior leaders to provide the vision for the organization's future. You have to start with the organization because the leaders will be part of that organization. That vision has got to be clear. It's got to be direct and it's got to be vibrant. And once you have that vision established and you know where your organization needs to go, then you know what is required from a leadership perspective.

Once you've sorted that out, then you have to do an assessment. First, you have to look at your current leaders, the key folks in your organization, then at those promising mid-level leaders, as well as being aware of those juniors that show promise to be groomed for the future leadership of the organization. When you conduct the assessment, it is very important to look at their skills, their knowledge, and their passion for what they do. You also need to look at their prospects for retention. So, for example, you might have some senior leaders in an organization who are just phenomenal, but will be retiring soon. This will drive the need to put serious thought in how you will replace them.

So you need to identify your key, senior leaders, determine how long you are going to have them, and to evaluate the current emerging group of leaders. When the assessment is complete, you are likely going to see that some gaps exist. Some shortfalls in the kind of leadership the organization is going to require will show themselves based on the vision that you've laid out. Some gaps can be filled by providing training and education to existing leaders to provide new knowledge and skills, which will require you to figure out who needs what. Some gaps will still remain, so you will need to figure how to recruit new prospective leaders both at the junior and mid-levels. Some needs will likely require fresh perspectives and skill sets at the senior leader levels, as well.

So this first assessment phase will address such questions as: what is the future of the organization?

Where is it going? What kind of leadership will that require? To what extent will the current leadership and upcoming leaders in your organization be the right mix and number to fulfill that vision? What gaps do I have? What do I need to do to address those gaps? Are there training education gaps for existing people or do we recruit new people? It's incumbent upon the senior leaders to develop and set the climate that's going to retain the existing key talent and is going to attract new talent. And I will submit that the way you do that is to come back over and over to the vision you set for the organization, because scripture says that without vision, the people perish. It is vital that folks in the organization or folks that are considering joining the organization have a very clear sense that the senior leadership has clearly laid out where they are leading the organization. You must make that organizational vision dynamic and vibrant such that current employees are truly excited about coming to work, and prospective employees will want to join you. I believe you can do that. You create a climate where you let emerging leaders learn. You find out what their vision is for their particular piece of the organization and you let them run it and you support and encourage them in doing that. So those are really the key things: having a vision, assessing leadership needs, and developing a supportive climate that will retain who you have and attract who you need.

At some point leaders, whether they be senior or mid level leaders, are going to start looking out across the landscape to seek out those individuals that may be those emerging leaders, people who can step up and begin to be groomed. There may also be

others who are great contributors but are not interested in stepping into leadership positions. When looking out at individuals, what would you want to see, what would you hope to see in an individual that will cause you to believe that he or she is someone that you can raise up into leadership?

The key thing I look for first is desire, somebody that really wants to be a leader. When I commanded the Military Intelligence Readiness Command, I needed an Active Guard/Reserve (AGR) officer to be the initial commander of an Army Reserve interrogation battalion that needed to be built from scratch, trained, and prepared to deploy to Iraq within two years. This was among the most difficult challenges I'd ever assigned to anyone. None of the officers presented to me on the standing command list represented what I knew I needed. So I did some homework and found someone serving in an ROTC assignment who was just below the command list cut. I called him under the guise of getting to know more about my up and coming Lieutenant Colonels, and spoke with him about his view on command and his desires for the future. His very first words expressed great disappointment about not being selected for battalion command. His passionate belief was that the officers should lead and command. And he was truly heartbroken about not having the privilege to do so. I knew instantly from that conversation that I had found my commander. I was able to get him assigned as the commander, and he proved to be superb, achieving mission success that most would have considered impossible. He later commanded as a colonel in an extremely challenging assignment. He never let me down, and was revered by his Soldiers.

Where do you see organizations missing the mark today when it comes to raising up those next generation of leaders?

It is vital that organizations identify and raise up that next generation of leaders. What I have seen all too often is organizations focusing too much on the here and now, and sacrificing the all important task of leadership development to achieve better results now. This is not an "either/or" situation. Both are important to an organization's future, and there is art to balancing them. You've got to give these emerging leaders responsibilities. You've got to give them freedom to fail. You have to give them freedom to try out new ideas. Yes… there are some unknowns, and there is some risk. Sadly, I have seen instances where current leaders are not willing to take that risk because they feel it could have some negative impacts on their own future career development or how their organization is perceived.

The culture of an organization can sometimes hinder development. What would you say to organizational leaders about helping them move the culture in the right direction so that it would enable people to move away from these fears and allow them to learn from their mistakes?

Sometimes organizations fail to recognize the changes that are happening around them and also fail to put in place adaptive mechanisms and a mindset within the organization to address these changes. The culture must show that it values leadership development. If that is not present, people will begin to see that there is no viable future and will be tempted to look elsewhere. Another cultural factor is that you as a senior leader must show that you are open to new ideas and that you are open to input from those junior and emerging leaders within the organization. So you've got to have an open culture that puts primacy on openness, that considers the worth of an idea on its own merit and not just on the status, rank, or seniority of the person putting forth the idea. The military struggles with this because of its formal rank structure, but no hierarchical organization is immune. But new social pressures have moved some senior leaders in new directions. For example, some general officers and commanders now utilize social media for more effective collaboration and to receive input from anyone throughout the organization. This is very positive step in the right direction.

Let's discuss sharing knowledge. Some people hold on to knowledge because they consider that their power. They don't want to share it because they want to be in control. Others want to share the knowledge because they fundamentally realize how important that is. I'd like your thoughts on the aspect of equipping new leaders through effectively sharing knowledge.

Most importantly, the senior leaders in the organization must be transparent. One way is through mentorship. I've always worked hard to accomplish this. I work to be transparent with those I am mentoring, to bring them alongside and discuss issues and challenges openly.

I will share what my challenge was, the decision I made to address it and why I made the decision. If I knew that I was going to get the microphone stuck in my face, I wanted to be able to say boldly that this is what I did and this is why I did it and, in the same circumstance, I would do the same thing again. Too often we don't share what we know. It comes back to that kind of competitive situation people see themselves in, that knowledge is power, and to share knowledge with others gives up competitive advantage. It's so easy to fall into that trap. It could be a commander at any level, or it can be leaders in organizations within the intelligence community. It can be individually or it can be organizationally.

I think there are four things you need to do to ensure that sharing knowledge becomes a part of the corporate culture. As a senior leader, first of all, you describe the vision with its goals or objectives. You clearly state what you are looking for. Then you need to resource it. This is where social media and other collaborative knowledge sharing technologies come into play. Then you demand that it will happen. When you don't see it happening, you take corrective action. Most importantly, you as the senior leader must model it so the folks can see that it's important to you.

Our society and culture are moving fast today. This is impacting how people manage their resources and prepare the next leadership generation. What would your thoughts be on how leaders can prepare themselves with those kinds of challenges today?

We know that there are economic challenges, that there will be new technologies that will force us to adapt as organizations and as people. We know that change is inevitable. We know that major challenges and even crises are inevitable. But we don't know exactly what they are going to be. So I would say the most important thing is for leaders to prepare themselves and their organizations to embrace change. Leaders must be more focused on fostering collaboration and mutual support within the organization. I used to tell folks when I commanded that change is coming and to be ready for it. But beyond simply being ready for it, you should actually embrace the change because, if you truly look forward to it as an opportunity to be creative, to innovate, and to overcome challenges as a shared team experience, then you're preparing the organization to become truly adaptable when change hits you.

Let me ask you a more personal question. We are all our own worst critics. We all tend to do so when we look backwards at our decisions and actions. If you could turn back the clock and examine some of the things that you did, the mindset you had, the ways you prepared, would there be anything that you might have done differently?

I feel very passionately about the collaboration idea, the idea of leveraging the full capabilities of an enterprise. I didn't do that or foster that or appreciate how powerful and important that was earlier on in my career. So I just wished I had the same passion years ago that I have for that now because I see the importance of it now more than I did earlier on.

If you were speaking with a group of leaders, people who you know have the charge to impact people with their authority, influence and decision-making, and you wanted to leave them with some key messages on leadership development, what would that be?

I guess that would come back to the primacy of setting the vision for the organization. The senior leader must set the vision. I know I've harped on that throughout the interview, but it is so integral. The vision is the organizing principle that brings unity of effort, prioritization, and synergy to everything the organization does. It also provides stability for navigating through change. Establishing the vision is not the exclusive property of the most senior leadership. Subordinate leaders, wherever they are serving within the organization, need to realize that it is just as important for them to set a vision that meshes with the corporate vision for their part of the organization. So leaders must anticipate change and prepare for that. But the truth is, we get busy with other things and preparation to deal with change falls lower on the priority list. So I would just ask this "Which organization will better weather the storm, and perhaps even thrive, when uncertain change occurs – the one that simply reacts, or the one that, through conscious effort and preparation, has a workforce both mentally and emotionally prepared to meet change head on, along with the requisite tools and skills to more likely achieve competitive advantage? "

Greg, thank you for your service to the country and for contributing to this very important

discussion. Organizations and leaders will benefit from your insights.

Kevin, it has been my honor and pleasure.

Chapter 11: Leadership Is About Trust...It Goes Both Ways

Glenn Webster
Former Commanding General
"Patton's Third Army"

Meet Glenn Webster, Lieutenant General (ret) now operating his own leadership development, training, and coaching business. Glenn is a 37-year Army veteran who commanded units in Kuwait, Iraq, Afghanistan and the United States. He is a successful leadership and management coach to the private sector, as well as to the military. One of the Army's premier trainers, Glenn has been called upon to coach and teach executive-level leadership by the US Army War College, NATO, and the Kingdom of Saudi Arabia.

A graduate of West Point, Glenn commanded at every level from platoon to division and field army. His operational experience includes assignments with five different Army divisions, two combatant commands, and twice with a field army and land component command. At the time of the September 11th attacks,

Glenn was serving in the Pentagon as the Director of Training on the Army Staff. Shortly thereafter, he became the Deputy Director of Operations for US Central Command, performing operational oversight for Operation Enduring Freedom, and throughout the CENTCOM area of operations.

In 2002, Glenn was appointed as the Deputy Commanding General of the Third Army, later designated as the Coalition Forces Land Component Command in Kuwait. During Operation Iraqi Freedom in 2003, CFLCC controlled all land forces in Iraq during the initial attack to Baghdad. He assumed command of the 3d Infantry Division in June 2003 and returned the division to the United States. Tasked with redesigning and retraining his division for a quick return to combat, Glenn led a team that designed the modular force used by the Army today. He returned the 3d Division to Iraq in January 2005, commanding the 40,000 US and coalition forces of Multi-National Division Baghdad.

Following nearly three years of command of the 3d Division, Glenn moved to US Northern Command where he served as the Operations Officer and Deputy Commander, overseeing the mission of homeland defense. In 2009, he assumed command of Third Army/Army Central in Kuwait, until leaving the Army in 2011.

Glenn is a graduate of the US Military Academy, the US Army Command and General Staff College, the US Army War College, and he is a graduate of the School of Advanced Military Studies with a Master of Arts Degree.

Glenn, thanks very much for being a part of this important leadership project. Let's move right into the discussion which is leaders raising up leaders. This is vital for any organization to continue to grow, whether it's military, private, or academic. As a senior-level leader, what do you see as the core responsibilities in making this happen and raising up new leaders?

It is important for the senior leader to understand and communicate his leadership philosophy. Philosophy may not be the best way to describe it, but it's been used for many years in the Army. It is critical that you tell people what is important to you and to the organization. It's describing the vision for the organization and describing how you want people to lead as they grow in the organization. My philosophy has three major points that I repeat over and over again. It has helped me build some high performing organizations and has enabled people to accomplish tasks that, at times, were levels above what they or others thought they could do. Standards are important for the organization and you set standards by words and action.

The second thing is to lead by example. It's one thing to talk a lot and give a lot of instructions. But I think you've got to walk the walk, not just talk the talk. If you want the organization to operate on a specific set of principles or values, leaders have a responsibility to believe that they are living in a glass house all the time. They've got to exemplify the leadership that they talk about.

The third point is that, once you have developed your standards, you must communicate how you want your leaders to operate at various levels. Once you establish standards, you must develop criteria by which to assess people. And you must ensure that these assessments are executed. If you are able to do it in a formal way, such as an annual or semi-annual assessment or a post-project assessment, that's even better. But, often we believe that our subordinates know what they're doing and they know how we feel about them. We overlook these assessments and move on. By doing so, we're missing a great opportunity to develop our leaders. Developing your criteria and establishing assessment tools to give that feedback in a formal or informal way are very important. Of course you can't leave it to your Vice Presidents or Deputy Commanders. You've got to get involved in the process yourself, again, leading by example.

There are some people who aspire to be leaders and there are others who are not looking to be leaders. For those who aspire to lead, what do you look for in that person to bring him or her along as a leader?

I look for knowledge, communications skills, character, organization skills, and responsibility. You also want to look at their technical expertise. Secondly, they've got to have the personality to be a leader. They must be able to embrace increasing responsibility and be able to give feedback to their own subordinates. They also must demonstrate the capacity to build a team, to organize for the missions. And they must be able to communicate well. Finally, strong positive character is required. They must possess good character. I believe it is important to focus on three things: mission, people, and teamwork.

Now 'mission' sounds like a very military word, but a unit mission is the same thing as the tasks necessary for your business to succeed. We've got to prioritize, because there's more to get done than any of us can get done in any given day. So, a leader has to prioritize those tasks, let them know your vision, your objectives, what you are trying to do in the organization. Make sure they all understand it. One of the ways to do that is to ask them about your guidance, and what they think about the vision or the mission or the priorities. Frequently seek feedback. We communicate but not well. We say something, we think it's understood, and then we walk away, only to find out later that someone is headed in the wrong direction. It may not be because they are obstinate. It just may be because they didn't understand what you said. So a good leader has a responsibility to make sure his subordinates know and understand what he's told them to do and what the priorities are. The priorities may change frequently. So you've got to give people the authority and power to come back to you for clarification. That sounds very, very basic, but I think it applies from the very senior all the way down to the junior-level folks. Mission and understanding the priorities is the first element of my philosophy.

The second one is people. This is where leader development comes in, in a strategic sense, but also the idea of helping people get ready for what's coming next. A good leader has the responsibility to prepare people for what may come next. Whether you're going to change the organization or about to cross the line and go into combat. It's the leader's responsibility to help prepare people for what is coming next. We've got to help prepare our juniors to take over and lead our organization or others like it and to take over positions of increasing responsibility. So the first two elements are mission and people.

The third one is teamwork. I really do believe that teamwork is vital, having played lots of team sports and also from a lifetime of service and leadership. If you build and sustain a great team, you can accomplish just about anything, even when it's extremely risky and it's extremely hard. If you concentrate on an overarching theme like mission, people, and teamwork, and we illustrate the importance of it and exemplify how to apply it, then I think your juniors will look on it in the same way. They start to realize if they are cut off from you in some military operation, can't talk to you, and are facing a dilemma, by referring back to the priority tasks of taking care of their people and maintaining a very good team, then they can't go wrong. I will support them in everything they do. I think it is important that we communicate that kind of philosophy, whatever it is for you and your organization, and then make sure they understand. You pat them on the back when you see them executing or doing things in accordance with that philosophy and you have an open mind and an open door to allow them to come talk to you about it. I also think it's important to give increasing responsibility. We want our juniors to be technically competent but we also want them to demonstrate self-discipline and the ability to discipline others and get the job done.

We should mentor as leaders, and help our juniors understand that we expect them to be technically competent, to follow our own leadership philosophy, and to seek out greater responsibility and authority. If they don't want to, then I think that's an open conversation we ought to be able to have with people.

You hit on a point I want to bring up which is this: In any number of organizations in the business world, these organizations are missing or doing things that hinder the process of leadership development. What have you seen organizations do or not do that either impedes or enables the raising up of the next generation of leaders?

Senior leaders are very busy people. They've got large organizations to run and obligations to meet. They may be in a life or death situation on literally a daily basis, or it might be the welfare of your organization's individuals and their families. The responsibilities are huge. We should take the opportunity to repeat that philosophy and vision and to tell our younger people how it applies. I can remember in a combat situation as we were planning an operation. The staff proposed a plan to me. For about a 30-minute back and forth dialogue, we discussed this simple philosophy of mission, people, and teamwork and how it applied. We applied this philosophy, something new and different, trying to keep it simple, logical, and flexible. I was able to refer back to those words numerous times during the planning. Does this contribute to sustaining the team? Does this do something to tear away at someone's authority and responsibility and reputation? Does this prepare people for what they have to do next? That kind of dialogue is something that takes a lot of patience and discipline for a strategic leader. Trying to find the opportunity to dialogue with those individuals several levels below us is something important and must be done frequently.

I also think that many of our subordinates, our young leaders, our potential executive-level leaders, have grown up differently than some of us, at least a generation or two different from us. It's not bad, it's just different. We've got to talk to them, create those dialogue opportunities to help understand and manage expectations. By managing, I don't mean reducing their expectations, but adding a heavy dose of realism. Make sure they understand what it is we have in mind for them. We must ask frequently: What's important to you? How do you live your life when you're not doing this work? How do you see yourself as a leader? Those kinds of things. Because if we don't, the dialogue breaks down and the team starts to break down. People think that you are out of touch. There are strategic leaders who are out of touch, or they're sandbagged in their office, or they travel way too much and they don't talk to the troops, the workers, the workforce, or the employees. That's another place where some organizations miss the mark; especially the opportunity to describe the vision repeatedly.

You should encourage people just below you to hand out increasing responsibility with lots of supervision. I don't mean telling them how to do things, but observing them as they grow and handle problems. Developing those leaders the way you want to and ensure they are not missing the mark. Morale and initiative can be seriously injured when visions get cross-threaded with actions.

This goes into another point I wanted to bring up about the culture. In some research I read recently, the Army was looking at this new young crop of soldiers coming in as "digital natives". This research has impacted how the Army strategically trains these soldiers. The culture, the environment, the means of communication has changed over the years. In reflecting on these changes, what would you point to as reference points as both senior and these rising junior leaders learn to address this changing culture and environment?

I think there's always been a little bit of awe balanced with skepticism with which our young subordinates look up at people at the very senior executive level. And there are some smart-alecs sometimes who don't consider it awe. They already think they know more than you do, and so they look at you askance. But all those subordinates of ours listen to us and watch us. At some point in time, nearly all of them will roll their eyes and wonder what planet we came from because the things that we know and say, the words that we use and the way that we talk about the world today and how it was... all of those kinds of things set us apart from our subordinates.

One of the important things we can do is develop this common language and just use it in the organization. Just use it when you are talking about what really matters to the organization. Those values, standards, that philosophy of leadership, the way you want plans and projects to be developed. If you were just to repeat those terms over and over again, a common language forms for the team. So I think we've got to make sure that the things that we do and say repeatedly take into account that somebody is always watching and always listening. You have to be disciplined to stay on message. And, if you find somebody who is violating your organization, you have to deal with it in a very serious manner. I didn't say "severe" or "harsh," but in a serious manner. It can't just be swept under the rug. Otherwise, suddenly you've set a new standard that is lower than what you had before.

The world is moving so much more rapidly today. You talked about communications and communication is happening so fast. Up and down, across different units in the military or different departments in business. And I'm sure you've been dealing with this yourself in the operations of your own business. How would you advise leaders who are rising up now to prepare themselves in handling and managing communications within their organizations?

Great point. And I'm not sure I've got that completely figured out with as fast as the world is changing, but I think it varies from different types of senior leadership positions. If you're running a military organization, a combat organization, or a supporting organization, it might be different from everything else. I think if you're running a large business, it may still be different. People have to recognize that they are living in a house with a lot more windows on it, at least, and maybe a glass house altogether. As senior leaders, we must realize that everything said in person or digitally can be used in multiple ways to help get things done, or to stop things from getting done right. We must be very careful. We must have advisors around us who have the authority and are invited frequently to question the ideas that we're coming up with in meetings, the things that we are saying as guidance.

I've found that having the right kind of leadership at the table, empowered to call a time-out in the meeting before bad decisions are made can be vitally important. If you think I'm headed in the wrong direction and about to say something morally, legally, or ethically wrong, then find a way to get that to me. Let's call a halt and discuss it so I can adjust where I'm headed. And I may not accept what they say, but they've got the authority to come tell me if they think I am doing something wrong. A lot of times it's prevented me from going the wrong way. It has reduced the risk. I think one of the ways senior leaders can do that is to have one or two people who can be fairly ornery, and are always looking out for your future and thinking about the worst thing that could happen, and helping advise you. What we put in our emails and in social media can have a disastrous effect. My advice to most senior leaders is to use social media rarely, very sparingly and let others communicate for the most part on social media. Anyway, I think we've got to have some advisors who are not our closest relatives or friends or yes-men. I think we've got to have people around us too who tell us when the emperor has no clothes.

You know, that's an awareness point that I've heard already from several other people. We have to be much more self-aware, and give people permission

161

to talk to us about our blind spots. I think that's vital, which leads me to a more personal question. We're all our own worst critics. We can look back and see things that we might have done differently. If you could turn back the clock and change the way you might have prepared yourself for the challenges that have come your way, for how you approached certain challenges, would there be some changes you would have made?

I think as a younger leader, I did not thank people enough for things that they did. As a younger leader, 20 years ago, mid-level manager, I expected everybody else to be as smart as me, as well-read, as well-educated, as well-trained, as intense, as caring as me. I sometimes expected all my teammates to do their jobs to the best of their ability, and that would be thanks enough. And I had people, a couple of times, tell me I was expecting too much of some others. The way I remember that it manifested itself was that I didn't say "thank you" enough. I didn't even thank family members: children, and parents, and siblings and all that kind of stuff, for things they were doing for me. People want to do what is well-received, they want to be well-liked, they want to be thanked for what they do and praised for it, and I just didn't see the need as a younger guy, and I wish I had.

I realized that I didn't say "thank you" enough to people at an earlier stage, and I now go out of my way to thank people for just about anything they're doing. And it's amazing how much better people feel and how in many cases, how much better they react, how much

162

better they execute tasks when they know that you've recognized them even with just a pat on the back.

And the second thing I think I'd do is I would have paid a lot more attention to the cultures different from mine: the cultures of countries we were going to be operating in, the cultures in a more detail-level of the people we were going to be partnering with, or that we were going to be fighting against, or that I might run into. The people whose culture in which we worked in the United States and of foreign areas. I knew it was important. But I paid cursory attention to it and I put my energies elsewhere. And I think if I could do it over again, that's one of the things that I would pay a lot more attention to. It has meant so much to us in this last 10 years to realize that we knew scarce little about our Arab partners, our Iraqi and Afghan partners and the enemies of both. And many things that surprised us shouldn't have caught us by surprise. Understanding the strategic environment is extremely important. Some leaders will have to designate somebody to help them understand that and to provide some special instruction and explanation frequently. I used somebody like that my last ten years in the Army and it was helpful.

We're coming down to a wrap-up here, so let me throw out one other question. It has to do with general advice to today's senior leaders. If you were talking to a group of CEOs, a group of senior executives in government, or rising flag officers, what would you want to leave them with concerning the raising up of that next generation of leaders? What things would you want them to not forget?

Our friend and classmate and the senior military officer in the United States, Marty Dempsey, Chairman of the Joint Chiefs, says leadership is about trust. Some people don't quite understand that it goes both ways. I think there should be a bond. We, as senior leaders, should seek a bond between ourselves as leaders and those we lead. There should be a bond of trust and mutual respect between leader and led. It's something you can ruin fairly quickly and it's something that, in some cases, might be fairly hard to develop. But it's important that we all think about it and try to develop a bond of trust and respect that goes both ways. We not only want to earn the trust and respect of subordinates, but I think we also have to learn to trust and respect them. You thank people. You coach them privately when something is not going well. You praise in public. You reward in public. You counsel and correct as discreetly as you can. You brag about them in public. You don't want to break down somebody in front of their peers and subordinates.

I think sometimes, in a very tough environment with high-tension, we eat away at the trust more than we want to. Setting standards and goals is critical for senior leaders. What are the standards that you want people to achieve? What are the goals and objectives for your vision for the organization? You've got to state those and lead by example. Repeat it frequently. And it goes without saying: mean what you say and only say what you mean. We have to be very careful about that as strategic leaders. Don't wander off into some area that's not critical to the mission. Don't think the mic is off, or that somebody's not listening, or tell an off-color joke.

Those things can ruin decades of work. The more strategic we get, the more we have to remember that old adage: the higher up the flag pole you climb, the more people can see your backside. We have to make sure we stay fully clothed as we climb up there. We should be disciplined to not get in trouble and ruin decades of work. Humility must accompany strategic leadership. Leaders ought to have a touch of humility and not think that they're perfect or untouchable by those under them.

I think that picture is a great metaphor for humility... its humorous, but its real, and people can identify with it. Now that you are in your new season after your Army career, what's the future for Glenn Webster? What are you hoping to do? What are some of the things you're chasing or going after now?

Well, I've decided to move to a peaceful, rural part of coastal Georgia where I have served our nation several times and where I have a number of friends and family. I am having a great time coaching and teaching leadership and leader development with Army leaders throughout the world and with private industry. And it's a lot of fun to learn as I go, but also to pass on certain lessons that I've learned over time. I'm going to spend a lot of time with grandchildren. And kind of make up for some of the time I spent away from my children as they were growing up.

Let me just say this in closing: I want to thank you first of all for your service. Let me also thank you for being available to participate in this discussion on leadership development. I'm looking forward to this impacting people in a real way

165

because I know many are seeking real people giving real ideas and experiences. So let me just end with that and say thanks for being a part of this.

Thanks very much for asking. I would also say in closing that we can never forget that these same leadership techniques and principles apply to our own children and grandchildren as they grow. We should be constantly looking at ourselves to make sure we are setting the best example for them too, because they are certainly going to be in charge in the future.

Takeaways

We trust that these conversations have provided you with a deeper understanding of the leadership issues and challenges that face anyone who has "charge" of any other individual. It does not matter how large or small the organization is. Nor does it matter if it is in the military, public, or private sector. Wherever there are people working together to accomplish a task, leadership opportunities and challenges will exist.

Whenever you have an in-depth conversation with someone on any issue, there will almost always be some "takeaways". We've endeavored to capture from these interviews those takeaways below:

Celebrate the opportunity in raising up others. Be diverse and go outside of your comfort zone. Do not just raise up people that look like you or with whom you are comfortable.

Subordinates will listen to you. They'll watch you and they will remember. You will plant ideas in their heads either on how to do things or on how NOT to do things. Rarely is this neutral. You either did it well or you did it badly and they will remember it.

People are the single most important asset that you have. Therefore, leadership is the single most important skill that can be brought to an organization. That means that leader development is arguably Job 1 in any organization.

Leadership comes in many levels and is different in each level. The skills, attributes, and abilities necessary to do each one successfully and optimally are different.

To the military audience, never forget the soldier and the impact that your decisions have on him or her.

To the academic audience, never forget the students…give them the foundational knowledge necessary to succeed in life and their careers.

To the industrial audience, always strive to thrill your customers with your product or service and set a goal to make the "100 best places to work" list.

Know the values of your organization. These are foundational. Never compromise on them. They include trust, teamwork, integrity, customer satisfaction and business success.

Developing a nurturing, collaborative, cooperative culture is job one. There is an accountability that's applied 24/7. You have to set that example. You know and everyone surrounding you inherently knows what right looks like. You need to live our life accordingly.

You and your team are in this thing together. You need to care about your individual team members as much as you care about the organization.

If you have a relationship with someone, you can solve any problem. If you don't have a relationship with them, everything is a problem.

Communication is a job that is never done. No matter how well you think you are doing it, you never can do it enough and you have to keep pouring on the effort and the communication.

Make leadership development a priority not just lip service. Leaders need to set the example. Leaders need to have a solid, well defined inclusive leadership development program that is clearly communicated to everyone. People want to feel special. That's why you need to treat everybody with respect and dignity.

For leaders who are growing, you've got to let them learn, you've got to have a system that lets them stumble. They need to practice and fail. You must instill confidence and develop the trust needed so they will succeed as they come up that chain. Everybody learns from failing and that is really essential for leadership development.

The senior leader must set the vision. The vision is the organizing principle that brings unity of effort, prioritization, and synergy to everything the organization does. It also provides stability for navigating through change. Establishing the vision is not the exclusive property of the most senior leadership. Subordinate leaders, wherever they are serving within the organization, need to realize that it is just as important for them to set a vision that meshes with the corporate vision for their part of the organization. So leaders must anticipate change and prepare for that.

Leadership is about trust. There should be a bond of trust and mutual respect between leader and led. It's something that you can ruin fairly quickly and it's also something that, in some cases, might be fairly hard to develop. But it's important to build that mutual bond.

Accept your responsibilities as a leader to prepare those who will come after you.

Concluding Thoughts

Being able to connect with people in an effective manner is vital to succeeding in any endeavor. It goes without saying that this is much more so the case for anyone who must pull together the efforts of two or more people to accomplish a task.

As I reflected on the relationships I have been fortunate to have developed over my life and career, I realized that I had come to know and develop relationships with people who possessed a rich background in the area of leadership and in influencing the next generation of leaders. Knowing how important this is to any organization, and with the encouragement of others with whom I have worked on some very challenging projects, I set out to capture these experiences and make them available in a manner that hopefully anyone can relate to. It was a privilege to be able to have these in-depth discussions with each of these men. Each of them would tell you that they are still in the learning mode when it comes to being an effective leader. The process is never-ending.

Naturally, conversing and working with these highly experienced leaders was not without a significant impact on me personally. So…I would like to leave my own "takeaways" with you:

First, becoming a leader starts with building effective, working relationships with people NOW…not tomorrow. If you are early in your career, doing this will serve you greatly as you continue to hone your own relational and leadership skills. This, combined with learning from the experiences of others, will bring tremendous personal and professional growth.

Second, you are number TWO in any relationship. By that, I mean that you must have the mindset of taking the first steps to bring value to that person or organization with whom you are engaged. This is counter-intuitive and even counter-cultural for many. But it is true. There is no lack of takers in this world. So be the one that purposes to give first. The impact will be significant with long-term benefits for YOU as well as for those to whom you are bringing value.

Lastly, I believe that each of us is created for a purpose. You can only control what you do through your God-given, free will. Make sure that what you choose to do serves your purpose…and serves those whom you are fortunate and blessed to influence with your life.

Need to Refine Your Team?

People may be communicating...but are they connecting...? Business leaders are challenged at all levels today. Based on recent research, consider what some leaders are facing:

- Learning to lead in the new era of connectivity and lateral communication among the younger workers
- Learning how to take advantage of the mindset of that young person who has been brought up in a culture of open communication and peer collaboration to address problems
- Moving their emerging leaders from good to great communication through connecting
- Maintaining core competencies for employees/team members/organizations in a cost effective way
- Helping emerging leaders/new employees to recognize their blind spots that may hinder their communications or collaboration effectiveness
- Building and maintaining a culture of responsibility and accountability with high standards
- Creating and implementing a leadership development campaign intended to build appropriate

competencies of organizational leadership for the future

- Keeping the organization competitive, accomplishing its mission, and surviving in times of challenging change

LMK Partners LLC will provide executives, senior business managers, and emerging leaders with tools that can effectively assist in facing these challenges through reducing conflict, improving communications effectiveness, and enhancing team cohesion.

Tools and resources include on-site case study-based workshops, one-on-one coaching, and focused assessments.

About the Author

Kevin Lewis is the CEO and Managing Partner of LMK Partners LLC, a veteran-owned enterprise. His firm delivers services in the area of organizational improvement, productivity analysis, and digital/print-on-demand publishing. His career includes service as a combat arms officer in the U.S. Army and 30+ years in the competitive world of information technology, collaborative study research, and management consulting.

In addition to managing the delivery of his firm's services, he has taken on the personal mission of working as a coaching partner with today's emerging senior business leaders. "The pace of today's business climate is causing many leaders to stumble, costing them time, money, and more importantly valued relationships. I want to bring my own lessons learned to the table to assist these leaders in becoming more effective and productive...and help them get a good night's rest."

Kevin is a Certified Human Behavior Consultant, a Board Certified Coach (Center for Credentialing and Education), and DISC trainer/facilitator. He received his coaching certification and DISC training through the Christian Coach Institute LLC .

He received his undergraduate degree from the United States Military Academy at West Point and his graduate degree in business administration from Central Michigan University in Mt. Pleasant, Michigan.

He is an author and speaker. He serves as an adjunct professor for the School of Business at Northern Virginia Community College and is on the Board of Directors for the Mount Vernon-Lee Chamber of Commerce.

Other Books

Reflections from the C-Suite:
Opinions and Advice

This book provides a conversational and candid discussion with 8 business leaders who have served or are currently serving at the C-Level of corporate America. It has reached #1 bestseller status within Amazon's Organizational Change category and # 7 in its Leadership category.

Voices from Main Street: Tips, Insights, and Advice
from Small Business Owners

Thinking of starting a business? Of being an entrepreneur? Looking for candid advice on the challenges involved? Need some tips on what you need to consider as you step out on such an endeavor? This book captures these perspectives from 9 small business owners ranging from a specialized cake connoisseur to an urgent care clinic owner to an IT services defense contractor.

www.ingramcontent.com/pod-product-compliance
Lightning Source LLC
Chambersburg PA
CBHW051501170526
45166CB00001B/336